COLLECTED POEMS

T0336284

COLLECTED POEMS

1952–1999

Robert Mezey

The University of Arkansas Press
Fayetteville
2000

22   21   20   19   18   5   4   3   2

Designed by Liz Lester

⊛   The paper used in this publication meets the minimum requirements of the American National Standard for Permanence of Paper for Printed Library Materials Z39.48–1984.

LIBRARY OF CONGRESS CATALOGING-IN-PUBLICATION DATA

Mezey, Robert.
  [Poems]
  Collected poems, 1952–1999 / Robert Mezey.
      p.   cm.
  ISBN 1-55728-612-4 (pbk. : alk. paper)
  I. Title.
  PS3563.E98 A6 2000
  811'.54—dc21   00-009640

In memory of Dick Barnes and Edgar Bowers

I se that makaris amang the laif
Playis heir ther pageant, syne gois to graif;
Sparit is nocht ther faculte. . . .

CONTENTS

THE MERCY OF SORROW
after Uri Zvi Greenberg

THE DOOR STANDING OPEN

INTERLUDE: Prose and Cons

SMALL SONG

INTERLUDE: Clerihews and Other Sports

GLOSSES AND VARIATIONS

COUPLETS 205

SOME OCCASIONAL POEMS

INTERLUDE: More Clerihews 249

EVENING WIND AND OTHER POEMS

FOREWORD

The arrangement of books in this collection is chronological. With the exception of my first book, from which I have taken only a handful of poems, the books are not appreciably different from what they were when first published—I have dropped or added a poem or two or changed the order slightly, and although I would not want to be too hard on that young poet of thirty or forty years ago, I have not scrupled to revise a little where I thought I must, and could. To the last section, *Evening Wind,* I have added a fair amount of more recent work.

I believe that the first verse I ever wrote was a translation at age thirteen of a passage from Ovid, and since then I have spent a large part of my literary life on this way of writing poetry, one way of many. I call it gloss or variation for the sake of greater accuracy; translation is a mirage, if not misprision. Long experience has convinced me that any poem put into English must be, first and last, a poem in English. Whether my poem has rung changes on or taken liberties with another writer's poem, or tried to carry over as much of its argument and figuring as formal commitments would allow, I value it as I would any poem I made, for whatever pleasure it gave me in the making and may give a reader. In the end they are all, for better or worse, my words.

I have had it on good authority that a serious poet should not write, or at least not publish, light verse and occasional poems, but as with translation, poetry is my way of life, and it makes very little difference to me whether I ply my trade at the mysterious promptings of a Muse or the directions of my answering machine, or because my daughter has commanded of me an epithalamion. (I should count myself very lucky indeed if I could write an occasional poem half as good as "Norfolk sprang thee, Lambeth holds thee dead" or "The Convergence of the Twain.")

My thanks to the editors of the journals, papers, and magazines, some no longer extant, in which most of these poems first appeared. I would have been at a loss with many of the poems originating in other languages without the plain-spoken criticism and suggestions of Ronald Cluett, Ben Zion Gold, Howard Jackson, Alicia Jurado, Ferenc Kalnay, Richard McKirahan, Eric Miller, Hardie St. Martin, Shulamith Starkman, and Donald Yates; and Dick Barnes gave so much to the imitations of Borges that they are, in every sense of the word, collaborations. Over the years I have had help from more friends than I can remember, but there are six in particular in whose taste and judgment I have the utmost faith and whom I have relied on to give me unsparing responses to my poems, which I have no doubt would otherwise be less interesting and less accomplished: Dick Barnes, Peter Everwine, David Ferry, Ronald Goodman, Donald Justice, and Miller Williams. They have always been generous with their time and energy, and they are not to blame for any of the blemishes to be found in these pages. This book is now on its own.

DEDICATION

for Donald Justice

To whom shall I give this skillful little volume,
Rewritten a hundred times, and mulled, and polished?
To you, old friend (and my teacher),
Who have always made too much of my modest talent,
You who, yourself the cynosure of our circle,
Have always been ready with praise for friends and students,
The while that you surprised and surpassed us all—
This book, for whatever it's worth. May it live for a little,
May it live to do you honor a hundred years hence.

after Catullus

from

THE LOVEMAKER

THE FUNERAL HOME

In the environs of the funeral home
The smell of death was absent. All there was
Was flowers rioting, the odors blown
Palpable as a blossom into the face,
To be crushed, to overpower—as if the grass
Already covered the nostrils in that place.

Hyacinths, larkspur, irises, flags of summer
Freshening and quickening in the little
Dawn breeze, and opening to a bee's clamor
The delicate parts, just now fragrantly ready,
And now beginning to die, the damp petal
Swaying a little with the weight of the bee's body—

Let them cut these flowers. Let them be ruddy
And sunlit gold and white and let them be
Heaped up and overflowing over the body
Waiting to be put down. To be unborn.
Something is sprouting in dark mahogany
Out of them—edged, and shining like a thorn.

1952

A BEDTIME STORY

Accidents will happen. Still, in time,
The rigors of mortality will chill
The piping channels of the blood and spin
Around the brain a cold and covering skin.
Then one might not remember pain so well;
One could sit back, and life, if not sublime,
Would be a sleep to dream pleasantly in,
Enlarging on the heroics of one's prime.

Nothing about longevity is heroic.
When he was eighty, Sophocles sighed, and said,
"This well loved instrument's finally out of tune.
Well, I am old, and have my work." And soon
Wrote *Oedipus Rex*, but in the night, in bed—
Well, it would test the most brave, the most stoic:
His genitals were wrinkled as a prune,
His nerves gone dull and every thought prosaic.

Then there was Stanley Ketchel, whose reckless love
And subsequent early death preserved his youth
And left his classic body middleweight slim.
Graceful and powerful we remember him,
His battering fists telling the brutal truth.
But there are countless tales. It is enough
To learn the fate of vigorous life and limb
And lose it young in grandiose rough stuff.

Ah, if only the dawn had thought to ask
For something more, for supple muscles, say,
An ageless heart to keep the flesh and blood
Robust as well as living for the good
Of her fair-haired boy, who came to hate the day,
The endless afternoon, the endless dusk,
That left him frozen in his fossilhood,
His deathless eyes bright in his bitten mask.

The specter of an old man's ugly phiz
Drifts in the gloom, wearing a dreadful smile.
Regard this silly ghost as he goes by:
Was he not thoughtless once as you and I
Of what must happen in a little while,
Who now despairs that he is come to this?
Shall you and I instruct him how to die?
Come close, come closer, kill me with a kiss.

DREAM OF DEPARTURE

Now spring comes back in green and blond,
And now the equinoctial gales
Are stilled by the genial western wind.
Catullus, leave the Phrygian paddies,
Sultry Nicæa's teeming hills;
Let's fly to the famous Asian cities—
Now the expectant, avid mind
Would wander and the feet move out.
Farewell, dear band of comrades, who,
Set forth together long ago,
Return by many a different route.

after Catullus

THE KILLING

We come for rabbit. Into a field
Snowgrazed and frozen hard we enter
With shells and loaded shotguns, chilled
To the bone, from woods stripped bare by winter
To the steep furrow picked of its yield.

Following dark necessities
We poke sticks in a small tunnel,
Or stop among broken stalks and freeze,
To bring this nibbler of leaf and kernel
To the mercies of his enemies.

All afternoon we walk and squat
And wait for the hoped-for death to happen.
A rabbit scampers across the rut
And tumbles hard as the bucking weapon
Empties its dead weight in his gut.

Grey trembling thing, the passive eye,
Bright in this tangle of shuck and tassel,
Seems asking what will come and why,
Up to the moment bone and gristle
Give to the gun butt's blunt reply.

All I can say is, what I do
Answers to something in my nature,
Some need that love cannot subdue.
I might have spared this quiet creature,
But hungered, and my aim was true.

A COFFEE HOUSE LECTURE

Come now, you who carry
 Your passions on your back,
Will insolence and envy
 Get you the skill you lack?
Scorning the lonely hours
 That other men have spent,
How can you hope to fathom
 What made them eloquent?

Blake tells you in his notebooks,
 If you would understand,
That Style and Execution
 Are Feeling's only friend,
That all Poetic Wisdom
 Begins in the minute,
And Vision sees most clearly
 While fingering a lute.

Robert Burns in Ayreshire
 With meter and with gauge
Studied the strict exactitudes
 That illuminate his page,
Ignored the vulgar grandeur
 That you and yours hold dear,
And labored with his body
 And his perfected ear.

Valéry gripped a scalpel
    And sweated at his task,
Bent over bleeding Chaos
    In spotless gown and mask;
And in reluctant lectures
    Spoke of the cruel art
And cold precise transactions
    That warm the human heart.

How many that have toiled
    At the hard craft of verse
Had nothing more than music
    To fill their empty purse,
But found it was sufficient
    In making out a will
To pay for their mortality,
    And they are living still.

CORINNA IN VENDÔME

Darling, each morning a blooded rose
Takes the sunlight in and shows
Her soft, moist, and secret part.
See now, before you go to bed,
Her skirts replaced, her deeper red—
A color much like yours, dear heart.

Alas, her petals blow away,
Her beauties in a single day
Vanish like ashes on the wind.
O savage Time! that what we prize
Should flutter down before our eyes—
Who also, late or soon, descend.

Then scatter, darling, your caresses
While you may, and wear green dresses;
Gather roses, gather me—
Tomorrow, aching for your charms,
Death shall take you in his arms
And shatter your virginity.

after Ronsard

DREAM OF AN INVITATION

Ipsithilla, my pet, my favorite dish,
Plump, wanton little coney, how I wish
You'd bid me join you for the noonday nap
And let me spend this scorcher in your lap.
How does that sound? Then see that man nor mouse
Opens your little gate. Don't leave the house.
Just change the sheets, break out your bread and wine,
And one by one, my puss, we'll tear off nine
And melt away in joy. Want to know how?
Then let me come immediately, for now,
Swollen with lunch and dreams, catching your scent,
I watch my tunic hoisted like a tent.

after Catullus

ON A THEME OF SAPPHO'S

That man seems to me almost a god, or even
—dare I say it?—surpasses the gods, he who
sitting turned towards you continually
      watches and catches

your dulcet laughter—all of which drains my senses,
for always when I turn and face you, Lesbia,
not a breath remains in my mouth, not a sound,
      nothing is left me,

but my tongue thickens and limbs melt, as a flame
races along nerve and vein, with a mute thunder
my ears ring, and my eyes go dark under
      wave after wave . . .

Idleness, Catullus, idleness weakens you.
From idleness you suck too deep a pleasure—
idleness, that has brought down powerful princes,
      prosperous kingdoms.

after Catullus

DARK HEAD

Dark head, your heavy sleep, the gift
Of passion loosed in the light an hour,
Remembers well what shadowy thing
Turned earthward in a golden shower.

Your mingled fragrances in sleep—
The breath of ferns, the breath of ocean—
The tangle of our arms and legs,
The cooling sweat of their commotion—

Move me to pray that time might cease,
That somehow I might shield from death
Our loosening bond, your hair, your face,
Changing a little with each breath.

Let me be chastened where you lie
Beyond possession still, beyond
The small cage of my heart, its sick
Persistence for eternal blonde,

And give these barren hungers up,
Love's shabby kinsmen. It is night,
And summer, and the wind is dense
With rain and questions. By what right

Can we two be as we have been,
Or ever pass this way again?
Breathe deep, dear heart. Another day
Is rising, and the wind and rain.

EPITAPH OF A FAITHFUL MAN

You of the covered breasts, the lovely head,
Must now be withered, or like me, a ghost.
Say that some women had of me a token
Of that long love which you alone could boast;
Say that I slept in many another's bed—
I sleep here now, my oath still unbroken.

THE LOVEMAKER

I see you in her bed,
Dark, rootless epicene,
Where a lone ghost is laid
And other ghosts convene;

And hear you moan at last
Your pleasure in the deep
Haven of her who kissed
Your blind mouth into sleep.

But body, once enthralled,
Wakes in the chains it wore,
Disheveled, stupid, cold,
And famished as before,

And hears its paragon
Breathe in the thronging air,
The lone, anonymous one,
Ravished by despair.

Lovemaker, I have felt
Desire take my part,
But lacked your constant fault
And something of your art,

And would not bend my knees
To the unmantled pride
That left you in that place,
Forever unsatisfied.

LATE WINTER BIRTHDAY

The lamps go out as if they feared the dawn.
Leaning drugged with sleep on the windowsill,
I watch the dawn wind waken the snows
To aimless forage. Somewhere, with measured blows,
A huge black bell is beating what is gone
Into the splintered forest of my will.

TO A FRIEND ON THE DAY
OF ATONEMENT

Impenitent, we meet again,
As Gentile as your wife or mine,
And pour into a jelly glass
A cheap, dry California wine.

Jewless in Gaza, we have come
Where worldly likenesses commence
To gather fury and still we keep
Some dark, essential difference.

Is it the large half-chiseled nose,
That monument to daily breath?
Is it some fiber in the heart
That makes the heart take stock in death?

God only knows. And who is he,
The cold comedian of our harm?
I wear its red stains on my sleeve,
You like a scar on either arm,

But neither knows what good it does.
The voiceless darkness falls again
On this elaborate wilderness
And fills the empty minds of men

Where they sit drinking with their wives,
Children asleep but not in bed—
Nothing to atone for but the long,
Blurred perspectives of the dead.

VETUS FLAMMA

That love that once was nearest to my heart
And pressed against my arm and forehead too
Is gone and you went with it. We are two.
You have your legends, I have an empty heart,
And in the quieted pounding of this heart
I hear the future I awaken to.
Night falls each dawn and stays a week or two,
And all there is to eat is my own heart.

I nurse a broken love, a broken word,
And cannot bring myself to say your name,
But keep the smallest remnant of your word
To ornament my door with what was lost.
Unaging ghost, you never said your name—
You only came to wrestle, and I lost.

THE WANDERING JEW
for Henri

> *Remember, I pray thee, who ever perished, being*
> *innocent? or where were the righteous cut off?*
> > *Teach me, and I will hold my tongue: and cause me*
> *to understand wherein I have erred.*

I

When I was a child and thought as a child, I put
The golden prayer-shawl tassel to my lips
As if I kissed God's hem in my child thought.
I touched the scroll with burning fingertips.

In my left temple was a shallow dent;
Rabbi called it "the forceps of His will."
I was a boy then, and obedient:
I read the blessings and I read them well.

I bound the arm and forehead in the faith
With the four thongs of the phylacteries,
Dreaming of how, when we were nearest death,
God brought the proud Egyptians to their knees.

Such were His gifts, the praises of Whose mercy
Fell on those years like rain and made them green—
What simple years they were! I loved Him fiercely
Who loved the Jews and smote the Philistine.

Leaving for evening prayers, I felt the breath
Of the hot street on my cheek, I saw a door

Alive with shadow, hips and breasts and mouth,
And thought, Is she one? with a thrill of fear.

I saw the buzzing neon. A black drunk
Holding his head together with a rag.
A squad car parked across the street. The bank.
A childish FUCK chalked on the synagogue.

The great doors took me in, as in a dream.
A darkness held the muttering congregation,
A voice in darkness crying *Elohim!*
And a listener crying, drunk on sweet emotion.

II

I cannot now remember when I left
That house and its habitual old men
Bowing before the Ark. I was adrift,
And much in need of something I had seen.

At morning and at evening in my mind
A girl in sheer silk over nothing on
Smiled with her eyes and all the while her hand
Played at closing and at opening her gown

And touched herself at length; her touch was sure.
It was not long, I ached for her, and acted,
And found one like her, although not as pure;
I liked the real as well as I expected.

I burned for it, both married and unmarried,
And either way I sometimes slept alone,
But either way, above the headboard tarried
Always a Presence that would not be gone.

Or so I thought. Leaving a girl one night,
I saw how my whole life had been arranged
To meet His anger in a traffic light,
And suddenly I laughed, and the light changed.

And the next night, obedient to my nature,
My head was filled with dew as we leaned to kiss.
Why should I leave my Egypt? To be some creature
Wandering unslaked in the wilderness?

I sucked for milk and honey at her tongue,
I strained against her, though we moved alone,
And still I heard a voiceless questioning
As I lay by her body in the dawn.

I lay unmoving in the small blue light—
What were the years then but the merest ash,
Strewn by a breath? And what half-buried thought
Fastened its pincers in my naked flesh?

Rabbi, I came, pounding with reddened knuckle
On the locked door, demanding whether the Lord
Lived in this vacuum of the Tabernacle
Or had departed, leaving only His Word?

III

For years I ate the radish of affliction
Until my belly sickened of its tang.
The sparks flew upward while my old affection
Sagged with my arguments of right and wrong.

The homeless swarmed on the stone hills of the city,
Armed children sacked each drowsy neighborhood,
And I who had seen with nothing more than pity
Saw beast and angel mingling in their blood.

Tasting my bondage in the lives of others,
I found it bitter, indigestible food.
If all the wretched of the earth were brothers,
Where would I find our father in my God?

I could find rest until a dream of death
Flooded the mechanism of my heart:
Nightly now, nomads with broken teeth
Come mumbling brokenly of a black report.

Reeking of gas, they tell what ancient fame,
What mad privation made them what they are,
The dead, the dying—I am one of them—
Dark-blooded aliens tagged with David's star.

A flock of people prey to every horror,
Shattered by thirty centuries of war,
The sport of Christian duke and *Hauptsturmführer*—
Is this the covenant we were chosen for?

Sometimes, at noon, the dull sun seems to me
A *jahrzeit* candle for the millions gone,
—As if that far, indifferent fire could be
Memorial to one blackened crumbling bone!

Tempted and fallen, the Lord God is brooding
Over the ashes where Job sat in pain,
And yet His tribe is ashes, ashes bleeding
And crying out to the sun and to the rain.

I speak of those that lived by rope and spade,
Of those that dug a pit for friend and brother
And later lay down naked in its shade—
There, at last, the prisoners rest together.

I speak it in an anguish of the spirit.
What is man, I ask—and what am I?
One who is one of many to inherit
A barren mountain and an empty sky.

It is a modern habit of the mind
To look at flesh and tear its clothes away,
That makes consoling speech a figment of wind,
Deliverance like something in a play.

The nights are darker than they used to be.
A squalid ghost has come to share my room.
And every night I bring him home with me—
If one can call dissatisfaction home.

All week long I have read in the Pentateuch
Of how I have not lived, and my poor body

Wrestled with every sentence in the book.
If there is Judgment, I will not be ready.

The book I read last night will be my last;
I have come too far lacking a metaphysic.
Live, says the Law—I sit here doing my best,
Relishing meat, listening to music.

INTERLUDE:
THE BALLAD OF
CHARLES STARKWEATHER

[To the tune of "Once I Had a Pretty Girl"]

He was just a young Nebraska boy,
His hair was fiery red.
His father gave him a gun for a toy—
    "What's your hurry?" Charlie said.

He shot eleven men for play
And left them there for dead,
And when they tried to crawl away,
    "What's your hurry?" Charlie said.

His girlfriend watched him burn them down,
She watched them while they bled.
"Oh, Charlie, give them another round!"
    "What's your hurry?" Charlie said.

He shot her father while he ate,
Her mother in her bed.
Carol cried out, "Let's celebrate!"
    "What's your hurry?" Charlie said.

Young Jensen was sitting in his Ford
With the girl he was soon to wed.
Charlie stepped up on the running board—
    "What's your hurry?" Charlie said.

"Don't shoot, don't shoot!" young Jensen cried,
And his voice was full of dread,

As he tried to get out the other side—
    "What's your hurry?" Charlie said.

They stole a car and headed west,
Into Wyoming they sped.
"Oh, Charlie, won't we ever rest?"
    "What's your hurry?" Charlie said.

The twelfth man had a gun of his own.
He aimed it at Charlie's head.
"I'll give you two seconds to drop that gun."
    "What's your hurry?" Charlie said.

They brought young Charlie into court
To pay for the blood he shed.
The jury said, "Your time is short."
    "What's your hurry?" Charlie said.

The hot rods drove up in a crowd
While he was being fed.
They turned their radios up loud.
    "What's your hurry?" Charlie said.

They came for him at 12:04
And quickly shaved his head.
They hustled him down to the death house door—
    "What's your hurry?" Charlie said.

He sat in the chair; they strapped him in;
The weight in his chest was like lead.
The warden signaled to begin—
    "What's your hurry?" Charlie said.

Carol lay in her prison cell,
Alone on her narrow bed.
"Oh, Charlie, I wish I was down with you in hell!"
    "What's your hurry?" Charlie said.

WHITE BLOSSOMS

Neither descendant nor lucky ancestor,
neither relative nor acquaintance,
I am of no one.
I am of no one.
I am, as every man, nobility,
North Pole, mystery, strangeness,
and a distant light,
a distant light.

But oh God, I can't take it any more!
I would like to reveal myself
so that you may see me,
so that you may know me.
For this, everything—
self-torture, song—
I want to love and be loved and belong to someone,
and belong to someone.

                              after Ady

THE END OF AN OUTING

Leaving the pond, she looks like something I know,
hauled-up and dripping, glistening in the sunlight,
and swinging her heavy auburn hair she comes to the blanket.

Her eyes are on the trees of the horizon.
I stare at her shoulder and arm,
flushed, and palely freckled, and moist, and cold to the touch.

Behind the pines and cedars the sun is falling,
casting their shadows deep on the empty beach
and the cold red water, suddenly unfamiliar.

In a few minutes, she will undress and sit
alone on the gritty bench of the bathhouse in semidark,
slowly wiping her breasts with a damp towel.

AFTER HOURS

Not yet five, and the light
is going fast. Milky and veined
a thin frost covers the flooded
ruts of the driveway, the grass
bends to the winter night. Her face
is before me now; I see it

in the misted glass, the same
impossible smile and I can feel
again on my bare shoulder
the dew of her breath. We made
a life in two years, a sky
and the very trees, lost in thought.

I know what it is, to be
alone, to have asked for everything
and to do without, to search
the air for a face that slipped away,
to wait, and what it exacts.
I don't fear it, I say,

but I do, and this night
the wind against the window
and the top branches thrashing about
enter my life and I see
the coming time loose and dark
above me, with new strength.

YOU COULD SAY

Yesterday rain fell in torrents,
stripping the branches of leaves and
deepening the arroyo. Now,
although the sun glances like flint
at the edges of cars, houses,
antennas, the water remains.
It lies in the hollows of rocks
and in ponds on the roads. Last night
signaled a great change; today
winter breathes at my window and
a few last flies, stunned by cold
into fearlessness, nestle close
to my skin. Summer is burned out.
Why does this season with its joy
in killing and its sweet iron breath
always find me alone? You could say
but you won't, and I am slowly
drifting away, I am growing
oblique like the sun, striking out
feebly at what is gone.

                My love,
it was my nature to want you,
lascivious, aloof, a body
fresh as new-fallen snow, and as
cold. Like other men in my
desire, I asked for it and now
I have it—the wind, the black trees,
scum of ice on the roadside pools—
all that the rain promised, and more.

A NOTE SHE MIGHT HAVE LEFT

Sorry I couldn't give you the details
      or say goodbye;
   but if you feel beguiled,
it was your nature to turn a blind eye.
Only children believe in fairy tales
      and you're a child.
   And everything you had me say
      I said in play.

The play is over now, but still you stand
      on the empty stage
   where the great loves live on,
crying out to the darkness in a rage
that only the two actors understand.
      But one is gone,
   and all her speech was meaningless.
      So was the kiss.

NO COUNTRY YOU REMEMBER

But for the steady wash of rain,
The house is quiet now. Outside,
An occasional car moves past the lawn
And leaves the stillness purified.

I find myself in a dark chair
Idly picking a banjo, lost
In reveries of another time,
Thinking at what heavy cost

I came to this particular place,
This house in which I let my life
Play out its subterranean plot,
My Christian and enduring wife.

What if I paid for what I got?
Nothing can so exhaust the heart
As boredom and self-loathing do,
Which are the poisons of my art.

All day I resurrect the past.
This instrument I love so ill
Hammers and rings and, when I wish,
Lies in its coffin and is still.

I dream of winter mornings when
Between bare woods and a wrecked shack
I came down deep encrusted slopes,
A bag of dead birds at my back,

Then let my mind go blank and smile
For what small game the mind demands,
As dead time flickers in the blind
Articulation of my hands.

I know you must despise me, you
Who judge and measure everything
And live by little absolutes—
What would you like to hear me sing?

A strophe on the wasted life?
Some verses dealing with my fall?
Or would you care to contemplate
My contemplation of the wall?

I write from down here, where I live.
In the cold light of a dying day,
The covered page looks cold and dead.
And—what more is there to say

Except, you read this in a dream.
I wrote nothing. I sat and ate
Some frozen dinner while I watched
The Late Show, and the Late Late.

THE FRIENDSHIP

I

What we looked for always remained
in the blue haze drifting behind
our wheels, into the distance.
But our motors roared in concert;
we went into the wind,
faces distended by the wind,
drinking and mouthing in a kind
of brute ecstasy and thirst.
Deafened, with chinese eyes,
we asked what there was to ask
of the onrushing fields, of
the blurred white lines arrowing past
and turned to look at each other,
helmeted, strange, and apart.

2

In the late spring we looked for
snow, and found it in long
rounded patches under the pines.
It was cold in the sunlight
at that height, as we straddled
warm metal and smoked, facing
the timbered slopes where the winter
had come to pass. Down below
the river rushed green and white

over the rocks, and a hawk
floated overhead. Each was there
for the other, and our cheeks burned
in the raw piney darkness
as we raced the downward turns
between big trees, heading home.

3

Tonight the kitchen is warm
and brightly lit and quiet.
I drink his whiskey, he buys
my silence and delicacy.
He drinks and his tongue grows loose.
He loves me up with his lies.
The night cannot end unless
he spills himself, breaks a glass
or falls down, his agony
almost visible, like fumes.
When I reach out to touch him,
there is the empty chair
and bottle and he is wheeling
drunkenly round this banked
narrowing space, as if his feet
could say what it is he feels,
or his wet face. I can't speak
or think of what he must want,
and his eyes behind sungoggles
turn on me like a blind man's
fervent and terrified—

there is an animal loose
in this house, ripe with the scent
of mania, murderous, bloody,
full of blame, a grown creature
walking at last and beyond his power
to love, pacify, or kill.

NIGHT ON CLINTON

The bar is closed and I come
to myself outside the door,
drunk and shivering. The talking
champions, the bedroom
killers, the barroom Catholics
have all drifted away and I
am standing in a yellowish
wound of light. Above the blur
my breathing makes on the glass,
I look down the darkened bar
where the bottles are out of breath,
the stale tumblers bunched, and white
webs shriveling in the pitchers.
The plastic stools turn
in the hot light that bubbles
from the big Sea Bird, silent now,
and a shape vaguely human
moves with a rag and a limp
among the tables
piled high with surrendered chairs.
Nailed on the back wall, a great
Canadian elk fixes me
with his glazed liquid eyes and
the last lights go out. What I see
seems important now, but I see
only the dim half-moon
of my own face in the black
mirror of space, and I lay

my cheek against the cold glass.
Snow is beginning to fall,
huge wet flakes that burst from
the darkness like parachutes
and plunge past the streaming light
and melt into the street. Freeze,
die, says the veteran wind
from the north, but he goes on
with his work, the night, the snow,
and was not speaking to me.

Iowa City, 1957

THE NEXT THING IS ALWAYS ABOUT TO HAPPEN

A wire arrives, *We hope to arrive tomorrow,*
can you meet us in King of Prussia?
Or, *I owe too much money.* Always the new word
like an old action carried into someone's hands

and he is reminded suddenly of his life.
It is late morning, perhaps, cool and limpid,
the breezes damp with honeysuckle. *Six months now*
and I still can't remember she's not in the house somewhere.

So many lives are like pages I read in a book,
but the pages are torn and lost. Life goes on.
A bus exhales in the echoing terminal,
a face swims to the glass from the dark interior.

In the middle of sleep where they will enter unbidden,
the flags are snapping, the garbled message
burns on the wind: *our city in flames, in ruins,*
and the dead are straggling home with their red brows.

Whatever I think of is fingers that stretch toward me,
thin bones in a filthy envelope of flesh,
and I am a strong man, as strength goes,
my weakness swelling in every joint and gesture.

Our need reaches stubbornly down with a chancellor's hand
and we are equally gripped. Day after day
there is silence in King of Prussia
and thin black plumes of smoke hanging over the land.

BACK

Tonight I looked at the pale northern sky
Above the city lights, and both the stars
And the lamps of men faded and burned by turns,
Breathed in and out. You would have liked it here,
The emptiness, the wind across the fields,
And the spring coming on—especially
The strange white almond blossoms, their unfolding
When a car swings down the lane towards the orchard
And turns its headlights on them. Hard as it was,
I forced myself to think of everything
You liked best, the years before you died
In a locked room in an army hospital.
Or was it after that, in a southern city,
Watching the traffic lights go on and off
And the big-finned cars swim past in a blur of rain?
I know your heart stopped once when, slightly drunk,
Holding your daughter's hand, you stood before
The cage of a small, shuddering European bear.
That spring in Half Moon Bay, where the sad surf
Felt up and down the beach with endless sighs,
And in the morning the brown seaweed lay
Like old surgical tubing. It could have been
Any one of a hundred times and places.
But last night, opening your eyes from sleep
To the steady courtyard light, I heard your breath
Coming and going like a wounded thing
That would not die. It could have been
Nothing but mine, persisting one more night.

IN A LITTLE PARK IN FRESNO

I used to come here and sit on the rope
and alloy patio chairs and study my blank
passbook. There was my whole future
to think of, and I thought of it, sitting there.
After a while, I went elsewhere to sit;
but sometimes, passing late in the afternoon,
slowed by heavy traffic, I could see
others sitting and reading, deep and immobile
in the spidery chairs, as if they heard
above the swish of tires the palms breathing.
It's a nice place to sit, this time of day,
and I've come back. In the last light before
the neons of the avenue come on,
the tropical garden shudders at the edge
of green and shades into blackness. What now,
I ask, and for all answer
the bamboo rustles in the evening and sighs.

LOOKING

There are brown weeds bent down hard in the steady blow
And mustard and winterberry, magnified, bright in the wet,
There are fields blurred away to a slowly dissolving horizon
As I drive on the glassy black road, going home.
Draped on the wheel, I stare at the three days' rain
And dim scattered lights drowning out in the early darkness
Of houses huddled patiently under their elms.
But tomorrow morning, a light sharpened on glaciers
Will stream from the sky between exhausted low clouds,
And the mountains eighty miles away will have moved
Close on the flat suburbs and grown wrinkled.
And all of this, the storming, the raw peaks
In the massive wheel of light, these are new signs—
I believe them as they would be believed.
In the rooms I come to, touched by so many hands
And tasted by other rains, I stand at the door
And learn how a chair endures its wearing away,
The dust balls at its feet, the dead lamp
Arching above, indifferent to them all.
There is a table, there is the black stove,
And somewhere a clock is beating.

        This is life,
The curls of blood clouding the toilet bowl,
Bound for darkness; and the crooked lines
The rain makes on the windows; and not least,
These hazel haunted eyes, this livid mouth
Buried up to the lips in drifts of white—
Day after day, the strange face in the mirror

Which I awkwardly shave and study with shy glimpses;
And all the while, the flaking roads and clouds,
The rain, the mountains, the weeds, and the cool light
That bathes it all, even the lamps and chairs,
Are reflecting a life more real than our own,
A life made of the truth, which might be known,
Only for a moment perhaps, and perhaps but once,
By keeping still, going unnoticed, and looking.

REACHING THE HORIZON

Once it was enough simply
to be here. Neither to know
nor to be known, I crossed
in the full sight of everything
that stood dumbly in sunlight
or drank the standing water
when it was clear. I called them
by their names and they were what
I called them. In the low glare
of afternoon I advanced
upon my shadow, glancing
at the grass unoccupied,
into the wind and into
the light. What I did not know
passed shuddering toward me
over the bowed tips of the
grass and what I could not see
raced sunward away from me
like dust crystals or a wave
returning to its yellow source.

This morning the wet black eye
of a heifer darkens with the
passing seconds, holding my gaze.
It has grown cold. Flies
drop from the walls; guinea fowl
roost in the sycamore. Old
dog in the corner, the day

ripples into its fullness.
Surrounded by eyes and tongues,
I begin to feel the waste
of being human. The rose
of the sky darkens to a wound
and closes with one question
on its lips, and the million
stars rise up into the blackness
with theirs. If I spoke to this
formerly, it was as one
speaks to a mirror or scummed
pond, not guessing how deep it is—
Now I see what has no name
or singularity and
can think of nothing to say.

The doe standing poised
in the deep rut
ribbed with shadows
of larch and pine

her brown eye
brimming with sunlight
among the leaves
turned and was gone

The spade that was plunged
into the earth this morning
stands facing its shadow
on the white fence

THE CAT

Abby is watching you, her green eyes
Closing and opening like a languid pulse,
And in the black narrow pupils your face
Looks back at you in miniature. Or else,
Yawning at your amusement, she uncurls
And moves like oil to another place,
Or vanishes, and as the minutes pass,
The uncertain stillness a green study knows
Throbs and enlarges in you. In her gaze,
Wakeful, impassive, cool, fastidious,
You will find only the lesser mysteries
That guard the great. And there is something else—
If cats are mastered, then her master sees
His subject in its metamorphosis,
Hackles erect, the unsheathing of the claws,
The abrupt curvature of the spine, the face
Twisted into estrangement, and he knows
What you knew as you stared into that glass-
Green corridor of time and empty seas,
Your brute jaw quivering. You are someone else.

THERE

It is deep summer. Far out
at sea, the young squalls darken
and roll, plunging northward,
threatening everything. I see
the Atlantic moving in slow
contemplative fury
against the rocks, the beaten
headlands, and the towns sunk deep
in a blind northern light. Here,
far inland, in the mountains
of Mexico, it is raining
hard, battering the soft mouths
of flowers. I am sullen, dumb,
ungovernable. I taste myself
and I taste those winds, uprisings
of salt and ice, of great trees
brought down, of houses and cries
lost in the storm; and what breaks
on that black shore breaks in me.

MURDERER'S WINE

My woman is dead, I am free!
Now I can drink all I want.
When I came home without a cent,
her yammering lacerated me.

I am happier than a king.
The air is pure, the sky is fine—
we had a summer like this one
when I first gave her some loving.

The violent thirst in my throat
would take, merely to be dulled,
as much wine as her grave could hold,
which is to say, quite a lot,

for I threw her down a well, then
when I heard her hit the water
kicked some stones down on top of her
—I'll forget her if I can.

In the name of our tender vows,
from which nothing can free one,
for the sake of meeting again
as we did in our first good days,

I begged her for a rendezvous
one evening, on a dark road—

and she came! She must have been mad.
But then, we are all mad, you know.

She was still pretty, even if
less lively—she was tired, and me,
I loved her too much. And that's why
I said to her: Leave this life.

No one can understand my mind.
Does even one of those blind drunks
dream, in the darkness and the stink,
of making a shroud out of wine?

That endless debauchery, tough
as iron machines, could never,
neither winter nor summer,
imagine such love, such true love,

with its black magic and sins,
its hellish cortège of fears,
its flasks of poison, its tears,
its rattle of chains and dead bones!

—Here I am, free and alone.
Tonight I'll be dead drunk or worse.
Then, with neither fear nor remorse,
I will lay my head on a stone

and I will sleep like a dog.
The coach with its big heavy wheels

or a wagon out of control,
dripping with slime, slurry or dung,

could easily slice me in half,
crush my groin or my evil head—
But I laugh, as I laugh at God,
the Devil, the Church—I just laugh.

after Baudelaire

MY MOTHER

My mother writes from Trenton,
a comedian to the bone
but underneath serious
and all heart. "Honey," she says,
"be a mensch and Mary too,
its no good, to worry, you
are doing the best you can
your Dad, and everyone
thinks you turned out very well
as long as you pay your bills
nobody can say a word
you can tell them, to drop dead
so save a dollar it cant
hurt—remember Frank you went
to high school with? he still lives
with his wife's mother, his wife
works, while he writes his books and
did he ever sell a one,
four kids run around, naked
36 and he's never had,
you'll forgive my expression
even a pot to piss in
or a window to throw it,
such a smart boy he couldnt
read the footprints on the wall
honey you think you know all
the answers you don't, please, try,
to put some money away

believe me it wouldn't hurt,
artist, shmartist life's too short,
for that kind of, forgive me
horseshit, I know what you want,
better than you, all that counts
is to make a good living
and the best of everything
as Sholem Aleichem said,
he was a great writer did
you ever read his books dear,
you should make what he makes a year,
anyhow he says, some place
Poverty is no disgrace
but, it's no honor either
that's what I say,
     love,
      Mother"

A CONFESSION

If someone was walking across
your lawn last night, it was me.
While you dreamt of prowlers, I was
prowling down empty lanes, to breathe
the conifer coolness of just
before dawn. Your flowers were closed,
your windows black and withdrawn.

Sometimes I see a square of
yellow light shining through the trees,
and I cross the grass and look in.
Your great body on the bed
is nude and white, and though I'm starved
for love like everyone, the sight
of your black sex leaves me cold.

What would I say to a squad car
if it came on its noiseless tires
and picked me out with its lights, like
a cat or a rabbit? That I
only wanted to see how people
live, not knowing how? That I
haven't had a woman in months?

Therefore I stay out of sight
and do not speak. Or if I speak,
I make small animal sounds
to myself, so as not to
wake you. And touch myself. What
I wanted to do was enter
and bend and touch you on the cheek.

THE UNDERGROUND GARDENS
for Baldasare Forestiere

Sick of the day's heat, of noise
and light and people, I come
to walk in Forestiere's
deep home, where his love never
came to live; where he prayed to Christ;
slept lightly; put on his clothes;
clawed at the earth forty years
but it answered nothing.
Silence came down with the small
pale sunlight, then the darkness.
Maybe the girl was dead. He
grew accustomed to the silence
and to the darkness. He brought
food to his mouth with both
invisible hands, and waited
for night's darkness to give way
to the darkness of day. If
he held his breath and his
eyes closed against the brown light
sifting down by masonry and roots,
he could see her spirit among
his stone tables, laughing and
saying no. When he opened
them to emptiness, he wept.
And at last he kept them closed.
Death gripped him by the hair and

he was ready. He turned and slept
more deeply.
            There were many
rooms—tunnels, coves and arbors—
places where men and women
could sit, flowering plazas
where they could walk or take food,
and rooms for the tired to rest.
He could almost imagine
their voices, but not just yet.

He is buried somewhere else.

TOUCH IT

Out on the bare grey roads, I pass
by vineyards withering toward winter,
cold magenta shapes and green fingers,
the leaves rippling in the early darkness.
Past the thinning orchard the fields
are on fire. A mountain of smoke
climbs the desolate wind, and at its roots
fire is eating dead grass with many small teeth.
When I get home, the evening sun
has narrowed to a filament. When it goes
and the dark falls like a hand on a tabletop,
I am told that what we love most is dying.
The coldness of it is even on this page
at the edge of your fingernail. Touch it.

WHITE BLOSSOMS

Take me as I drive alone
through the dark countryside.
As my strong beams clear a path,
picking out fences, weeds, late
flowering trees, everything
that streams back into the past
without sound, I smell the grass
and the rich chemical sleep
of the fields. An open moon
sails above, and a stalk
of red lights blinks, miles away.

It is at such moments I
am called, in a voice so pure
I have to close my eyes, and enter
the breathing darkness just beyond
my headlights. I have come back,
I think, to something I had
almost forgotten, a mouth
that waits patiently, sighs, speaks
and falls silent. No one else
is alive. The blossoms are
white, and I am almost there.

THE MERCY OF SORROW

after Uri Zvi Greenberg

THE HOUR

The hour is very weary, as before sleep.
Like a foundling child, just in my white shirt,
I sit and write in space, as on a slate—
    No matter, no matter.

Should the black cat come to the pitcher and lick
The remnants of milk and overturn the pitcher,
I will close my eyes to sleep, and sleep forever—
    No matter, no matter.

JOY

And what is joy? A going up
So as to come down harder,
Hurtling into anguish?

Yes, there's a bridge from sorrow to sorrow.
In the middle a bush bursts into flame,
A heat that dries up the tear
Gathering on the eyelash—

Until the rejoicer reaches
Across, to the other side.

WITH MY GOD, THE SMITH

Like chapters of prophecy my days burn, in all the revelations,
And my body between them's a block of metal for smelting,
And over me stands my God, the Smith, who hits hard:
The wounds that Time has opened in me open their mouths to Him
And release in a shower of sparks the intrinsic fire.

This is my just lot—until dusk on the road.
And when I return to throw my beaten block on a bed,
My mouth is an open wound
And naked I speak with my God:
                              You worked hard.
Now it is night; come, let us both rest.

LIKE A GIRL

Like a girl who knows that her body drives me to begging,
God taunts me, Flee if you can! But I can't flee,
For when I turn away from him, angry and heartsick,
With a vowel on my lips like a burning coal:
I will not see him again—

I can't do it.
And I turn back
And knock at his door,
Tortured with longing

As though he had sent me a love-letter.

THE GREAT SAD ONE

The Almighty has dealt bitterly with me
That I did not believe in him until my punishment,
Till he welled up in my tears, from the midst of my wounds.
And behold—he also is very lonely,
And he also lacks someone to confess to,
In whose arms he might sob his unbearable misery.

And this God walks about, without a body, without blood,
And his grief is double the grief of flesh,
Flesh that can warm another body or a third,
That can sit and smoke a cigarette,
And drink coffee and wine,
And sleep and dream until the sun—

For him, it is impossible, for he is God.

ON THE EQUATOR

How rarely Your mercy visits me,
My King, my Father;
And so, most of my days, I am Your wandering son
Who has cast his lot like a prophet
In the desert of his days.

And Your deliverance that comes to me then,
My Father, my King,
Is like a well that the wanderer came on at last,
When he had almost prayed for death from thirst
And the heat that shrivels the body.

And at times it is so sweet,
It is like a miraculous dream that You give
To the blind man in his agony, at night.
He dreams that his eyes are open and that he sees
The face of his wife and the dark gold of her hair.

But at times You make sport of me,
My Father, my King,
And I draw back, and grow small with loneliness,
Like the blind man awakened from his dream.
I gaze at my coming days, and I descend
Into the black abyss of my life, as the blind man into his.

THERE IS A BOX

There is a box and a coverlet, and a pair of black horses
Stepping forth heavily, in honor, of course, of the grief.
There is a spade, and a strong man, the digger,
White linen, and a girl who sews.

Adam is dust, the Rabbi must surely be rotting by now,
And what remains in writing—a doctrine of no death.
I speak of what feeds down there in the mire.
There is nothing in books, only a few words.

HOW IT IS

I hear the sound of affliction. They are weeping,
It seems—human beings, male and female.
Once I heard only the joy of those who were married
To the juice and sweetness of life.

There's no need to ask why they weep—it's clear enough.
If women are weeping, it's a sign of their defilement;
If men, what could it mean but the loss
Of great faiths as powerful as the earth?

Souls that go forth gaily on their wanderings,
Adorned with their colorful visions,
How wan they are, and shrunken, when they come back.

THE VALLEY OF MEN

I have never been on the cloudy slopes of Olympus.
In the living man's valley I grew with the bread.
Like other men, I drank the sweet water there,
Waters where cattle drank, whose flesh I ate.

The Queen's train my forefathers did not carry, amongst the Gentiles.
The King did not call them, either in sorrow or joy.
They were poor Jews, shining and singing,
Little more than the shepherd blows through his flute.

So I am pleased to carry myself from sorrow to sorrow,
As the shepherd his littlest sheep from pasture to pasture,
And he eats a few figs, to keep the breath in his body—

Red seamed are the ends of my days and nights.

ON THE POLE

Some clouds are rain clouds—
On my head like a mist the mercy of sorrow transpires.
It is good to command the boat of all longings:
Stop and anchor.

For here is the Pole—and joy is native
To the country of youth, garlanded with beauty.
It is good to descend, to rake in the remnants of honey
And the white milk—in the final place.

THE DOOR STANDING OPEN

I am putting my words together for whatever intelligence there may be in the world. There is no other reality among men than this intelligence . . . To be more than I thought I was—a sensation utterly new to me . . .

That power we had felt running in us and through us could not, in the nature of things, be acutely conscious of us as individuals. It must come rather as wind comes to the trees of a forest, or as the ocean continues to murmur in the sea-shell it has thrown ashore.

AT THE POINT

Travelers long on the road
stop here for water and for the view.
Their children run
through the young and old pines,
splashing in the needles
or chasing wild canaries, their
light cries
receding in the aisles of shade.

The light is so simple
and steady,
it is as if tiny beaks
had opened a vein of pure sunlight in the forest,
and the fathers and mothers
stand looking down,
their lives
jumping at the base of their throats,
and little words
unspoken for twenty or thirty years
cling to their lips like droplets of water.

In the valley the taut fences
stretch pitilessly to the horizon,
and all those who want to be someplace else
must follow them.
The hawks and owls crucified on the wire
have long since returned to their own country,
and the mouse trembles in ecstasy,
lost in the shadow of their wings.

HOW MUCH LONGER?

Day after day after day it goes on
and no one knows how to stop it or escape.
Friends come bearing impersonal agonies,
I hear our hopeless laughter, I watch us drink.
War is in everyone's eyes, war is made
in the kitchen, in the bedroom, in the car at stoplights.
A marriage collapses like a burning house
and the other houses smolder. Old friends
make their way in silence. Students stare
at their teachers and suddenly feel uneasy.
Some of us move slowly as cattle feeding,
oblivious, looking down, and others spooked,
rolling their eyes skyward, while the young
walk aimlessly all night and can't stop talking,
or sit in a circle naked, speechless, hallucinating.
Small children roam the neighborhoods armed
with silvery guns, gas masks, and plastic sticks.
Excavations are made in us and slowly
we are filled in with used-up things: knives
too dull to cut bread with, bombs that failed to go off,
cats smashed on the highway, broken pencils,
slivers of soap, hair, gristle, old TV sets
that hum and stare blindly, blackened light bulbs.
Bridges kneel down, cities billow and plunge
like horses in their smoke, the tall buildings
open hysterical burning eyes at night,
the leafy suburbs look up at the clouds and tremble—

and my wife leaves her bed before dawn, walking
the icy pasture, shrieking her grief to the cows,
praying in tears to the softening blackness. I hear her
outside the window, crazed, inconsolable,
and go out to fetch her. Yesterday she saw
a photograph, Naomi our little girl
in a ditch in Viet Nam, half in the water,
the rest of her, beached on the mud, was horribly burned.

TEREZÍN

In your watercolor, Nely Sílvinová
your heart on fire
on the grey cover of a sketchbook
is a dying sun or
a flower
youngest of the summer

the sun itself
the grizzled head of a flower
throbbing
in the cold dusk of your last day
on earth

There are no thorns to be seen
but the color says
thorns

and much else that is not
visible it says also
a burning wound at the horizon
it says Poland and winter
it says painful Terezín
SILVIN VI 25 VI 1944
and somehow
above the body on its bed of coals
it says spring
from the crest of the street it says
you can see fields

brown and green
and beyond them the dark blue line of woods
and beyond that smoke
is that the smoke of Prague
and it says blood
every kind of blood
blood of Jews
German blood
blood of Bohemia and Moravia
running in the gutters
blood of children
it says free at last
the mouth of the womb it says
SILVIN VI 25 VI 1944
the penis of the commandant
the enraged color
the whip stock the gun butt
it says it says it says

Petrified god
god that gave up the ghost at Terezín
what does it say but itself
thirteen years of life
and your heart on fire
                    Nely Sílvinová

NOLAN

Who will come leading a horse,
a gentle horse with the eyes
of a good mother,
who will lead it to Nolan
who is barely five years old?
Nolan climbs on the back
of a barren mare
whose eyes, though they brim with sorrow,
are painted eyes,
and pressing his small groin
to the stiff scrolled mane
he rides,
and the mare bucks wildly in her frame.
All day and all night he rides,
but if he had a sword,
a real sword and not too big
for such a little boy,
he would drive it into her
where the hollow entrails are
and saw at the ragged hole
till he reached the heart
that has never learned to beat
and cry aloud the tears
falling on deaf ears.

CALIFORNIA FAREWELL

Tonight,
in a torn shirt,
in the last of the daylight
I leave the road
to its distances, dove
that flies away into the sky.

I still see your car
getting small,
fatalist metal rolling, rolling
to the dark beat of poles,
fence posts,
that blurred strip which was the desert—
your eyes fixed
on the endlessly receding vision.

Why are you leaving? I feel
like a raw baby in my open red shirt.

But I see the sun
give up everything without a struggle,
burning itself
into that powerful line that has no memory,
horizon
dancing away in radiant acids.

Something is sleeping
just beneath the poor grains of the earth,
ear pressed to the silence.

Now
I can say goodbye,
in the privacy of the twilight,
in the darkness closing around me,
the petals of darkness
closing up for the night.

A PRAYER IN HIS SICKNESS

You brought me, Lord,
to these sun-punished hills,
this Academy
where I opened my eyes and my ears
to the peacock braying
and the peahen running over the fields,
where I bent to the grass my brother
sleepy and red at the close of day
and made my farewells.
You brought me, Lord.

You bring me now
to the mouth of my 33rd year
but I'm afraid to drink
of this black water.
Weak hands, weak heart,
liverish spittle, lips
shaped and bled dry by so many cravings,
my whole life at sundown dissolving into the grass—
I turn away,
and you turn away in despair.

Be with me now.
Don't let me speak with my painted tongue
to the ghosts of this world.
Let me put off
this heavy finery, let me put off my suffering flesh
and I will come down to meet you, Lord,
wherever you say.

GOING FOR A WALK AT NIGHT

It is very late.
Few stars are left and those blinking
Like the eyes of a sleepy child.

I feel with my hand
Under the ribs of the wind
But I can't tell anything,
I feel with my foot in the dust
But all I touch
Is the shallow roof of the dead.

Looking back to where I started
I see a door of golden light
Opening in the roots of the black trees.
There sleep
The children who are not mine,
The wife who is not mine
And my life.

The road is only a darkness
Between darker banks,
Weeds that turn in their sleep
And pillars
That go whistling off into the void.

Unmoving
In the autumn cold,
I stand a long time

Until time flickers

And goes out in a pool of darkness.

Smoke rises from my lungs

And disappears

Among the last stars.

GOING TO HEAVEN

She went on her knees in the dirt
thinking of nothing
lost in the crumbling blackness
kneeling above her shadow
preparing a place for bulbs
and the few seeds held in the palm of her hand.

Now gladiolus rises everywhere
perfect in sunlight
spreading straight green wings into the air
and green curls in the shade
that will be eaten.

And I have dug steps in the dark earth
that we may descend to them.

PISCES' CAR SONG

All night driving south
I carried your pure mountain water,
hearing it slosh in the invisible glass
in the darkness behind me, following
lights down the flowery tunnels of the night
and rolled past first pink derricks of San Diego
heading into the desert
toward the slowly kindling skull of Sierra San Pedro Martir.

When the sun burst up in flames I saw it
lightly chopping in the clear 5-gallon jug,
swaying past
cracked gullies round Yuma, the unliftable dead stones
of the Territorial Prison,
past black wings rising heavily on Highway 80
and a lone ragged black man
wilderness walker,
little puffs of dust pursuing his shoes—
north of Live Oak Springs I saw two white-faced steers
ambling in sage and long sunrise shadows
and remembered myself,
the dark face streaked with sweat—
among ten thousand acres.

Between Santa Ana and Hermosillo
I stopped on the side of the road, unstopped the jug,

and put my mouth to its mouth.
It was like drinking of you,
nearer than my breastbone and yet so far.

I hope you meet me Tuesday,
I have your pure mountain water.

THERE GOES GATTEN

There goes a man on a long journey
Hurrying toward the almost religious solitude
Of the middle of the night.
Many nights he sat
At the open window listening
Sadly to the shrill of the small insects

Grinding their prayer machines in the grass
And great branches bending endlessly
To the breath that visits only a moment
The mouths of the living—
Endlessly, and he covered his face with his hands.
Now it is time to go on.

POEM

I am looking for someone to speak in this poem
Someone not I
Who can say
I without blushing
With a veiled smile

The other voices all belong to me now
And I can't remember where I borrowed them

If you have something to give
Give it to the man who vanished into the rock
To the one who watches and speaks
Behind his mask
Without breaking into giggles

As for myself I mistrust
My name my face
My fourth eye
The shadow of my hands in which
Ants scurry to their deaths

I predict my own death
When all my poems will fly back into my mouth

Small crystals
Dissolving in the acid of truth

NEW YEAR'S EVE IN SOLITUDE

Night comes to the man who can pray
only on paper.
He disappears into paper
with his old mouth shaped to say no
and his voice is so tiny
in all these miles of silence and cold grass.

As I write
the fog has eaten away the mountains
the princely hills and the fields
everything but this house
and this hand
and the few feet of light it throws out against the dark.

I try to talk
to the drunken god who sleeps in my arms and legs
tell him god knows what
but what's the use he won't listen
or else he listens in his sleep

and the dead listen in theirs
up on the hill
up past the drifting
iron gates the dead leaves
listen and the frozen
water pipes.

And I know what to ask.
I know what I really want.

Nothing any more against the darkness
nothing against the night
nothing
in which the bright child is silent and shines very dimly.
Cover me with your arms
give me your breast
that will make me forgetful and slow
so I can join him in sleep—

Hurry down now good mother give me
my life again
in this hand that lives but a moment and is immortal
cover my eyes and I will see them
those companions clothed head to foot in tiny fires
that I said goodbye to when I first opened my eyes.

Give me my robes of earth
and my black milk

ONE SUMMER

My father coming home
from the factory
summer and still light out
the green bus at the end
of the endless street
the foul sigh
on which my father stepped down
walking slowly in the shadows
holding my hand
my father tired and frowning
eating his supper of potatoes
reading the *Bulletin*
news of the war
and columns of boxscores
my father singing lewd hymns
in his tuneless voice
stretched out full length in the tub
his calves hanging over the rim
his long penis resting
on the surface of the grey water

IN THE SOUL HOUR

Tonight I could die as easily as the grass
and I can't help thinking
as the light flickers along the finished blood-red boards
how just the other side of the fiery grain
the skull of the house is clapped in darkness

The joys of our lives tonight
the dance sweat the shining sidelong eyes
the faint sweet cuntsmells hiding in perfume

music from another planet

voices at night
carried across the blowing water

I AM HERE

for Naomi, later

I

I want to speak to you while I can,
in your fourth year before you can well understand,
before this river
white and remorseless carries me away.

You asked me to tell you about death.
I said nothing. I said

This is your father,
this is your father like water,
like fate,
like a feather circling down.

And I am my own daughter
swimming out,
a phosphorescence on the dark face of the surf.

A boat circling on the darkness.

2

She opens her eyes underwater. The sun climbs.
She runs, she decapitates flowers.
The grass sparkles. Her little brother laughs.
She serves meals to friends no one has seen.
She races her tricycle in circles.
I come home. The sun falls.

3

You eat all day.
You want to be big. "Look how big!"
you cry, stretching your arms to heaven,
your eyes stretched
by all the half-terrified joy of being in motion.

The big move clumsily, little love,
as far as I can see.
They break everything
and then they break
and a pool of decayed light sinks back into the earth.

Writing these words tonight,
I am coming to the end
of my 35th year. It means nothing to you,
but I rejoice, and I am terrified,
and I feel something I can never describe.
They are so much the same,
so much the sun blazing on the edge of a knife . . .

We are little children,
and my face has already entered the mist.

4

I hear you cry out
in the blackened theater of night.
I go in and hold you in my arms

and rock you, watching
your lips working, your closed eyelids
surge with the nightly vision.

    5

I get lost too, Naomi,
in a forest that suddenly rises
from behind my skullbone on a night of no moon.
Stars hang in the black branches,
great, small,
glittering like insoluble crimes,
calling me, over and over,
toward that thick darkness under the trees.
I turn, trembling, to run,
but it is everywhere.

    6

I wanted to give you something but
always give you something else.

What do you call it when it is underground
like a cold spring in the blood,
when it is a poem written out of naked fear,
and love, which is never enough,
when it is my face, Naomi,
my face
from which the darkness streams forth?

The petal falls,
the skin crumbles into dirt,
consciousness likewise crumbles
and this is one road the squirrel will not cross again.

I was here, Naomi,

I will never be back,
but I was here,
I was here with you and your brother.

IN THIS LIFE

Now the cup of grasses and down is cool,
the eggs cool, the throne empty
from which she would step down and growing still,
look out long toward the darkness.

One moist and terrible night, it came creeping
and tensing its jaws and it too grew still,
and then it had her,
and a small diamond of light opened in her brain.

I remember the eyes closed tight
against the final ecstasy of the teeth,
the weightless blood-beaded lump of feathers buried now
under the iris slowly eaten alive by the air.

Here is the father
blossoming on a twig,
to sing the song of the bleeding throat
on this day of crystal wind and young sunlight.

He sings the endless song
of irises wrinkling and wrinkling and becoming nothing,
road of fine sand strewn with fallen wings,
the mouse, the toad, the nestling taken in deep grass,

he sings of a diamond, sings
of the spokes flashing brilliance at the center

of the ceaselessly collapsing floor of bone,
and I wish I sang with him.

He sings the coldest truth
in this world where we remember the warm lies,
sings it and sings it
till it breaks at last into particles of light,

blossoms of mercy
in the midst of the holocaust.

AN EVENING

The sun blazing slowly in its last hour

A horse motionless on a knoll
His long neck and mouth plunged to the earth
His tail blowing in filaments of fire

Tuft of grass that bends its illuminated head over its own shadow
The grass sleepy after the long feast of light

And the new leafed figs dancing a little in the silence
Readying themselves for the night

An evening

Understood
By those who understand it not

WATCHING THE INVISIBLE

wind climbing swiftly the steep hillside
the grass rearing and plunging like an ocean

day of wind day of barely audible
music driving the seed heads crazy
thin bodies twisted and swaying and bent down flat

wind printed with fossils and jewels
wind uttering flashes of light
revelation visiting everything the same
the wind brushing my bare skin with its silk like a girl
going in and out of flesh as through a door—

when I climb out of the old frog pond
wind is there to meet me
certain cold
thoughts racing ahead of the sunlight
not of death—

no, but I think of the day sinking back into twilight
and the hands held up dripping with it
the hands held up
drying themselves in the wind

SONG

Stars overhead
A frog's grunt from the other side of the pond
Clear sound in the summer night

Ollie is asleep
My warm foxy girls curled up at my sides
In my lap the story of a king and his youngest daughter

The perfume of hair
Little Omi is breathing the pure breath of sleep

Eve moves to the open door
My senses are full
Of her slim young womanly body
And tinkling anklets

I am ready for sleep

Orion blows like a kite in the summer sky
I think I will climb up his tail
To freedom

I AM BEGINNING TO HEAR

a voice in this life I am living
every day every night
never before heard

speaking in languages
made of shifts in the direction of the wind
seeds fallen from an apple
feathers in the dust

there is a flight of arrows or is it light
turning the way things turn
after the sun only at different speeds

brilliant darkness as in the night when there is no moon
I must have known it once

as now
moving easily as a hand
among the fiery lights raining out of space
I know what is said but it is
dark untranslatable

a flower suddenly folding up
and rushing away into its ancient parchments

INTERLUDE:
PROSE AND CONS

Oh shit.

Now Proudflesh was the mumbler one mount of that knack of the woods and as such had some streamly impotent duties, among which were life, lividly, and the hirsute hole of happiness. So it come as no supplies that he was trod and found giddy of embracing Nurse Tundra around the waste until she is dead. Witch is why we are spectacle in such matters and hesitate to make a funnel incision.

Wants a pond a thyme, a wight rabid set out to sikh for wisdom. Sot high and low, yeast and vest, Donne & Bradstreet, but all he found was an alarmist incidence of boredom that threatened to break out into an academic. Licked into every cram and nooky but all he founded was a spool of thought that streamed to him the very hide of stupidity. Poured over thousands of ledges and testicles, knocked over banks, sang his muzzle into any crevice no matter how juvenile, and emptied at last into the Specific, to lead a rife old age of supreme contempt for the State.

The old man's mouse waters at the thought of buttery ragamuffins, sunbaked urchins. If only he could land his choppers in the firm white sighs of a young girl, perhaps he would not have to die. Such an old man is called King Leer. When he opens his mouse to receive the Host, hole continence are orphaned.

The Marines have landed on the Island of Langerhans. There was no resistance. Their obstructions are to kill everything that movies. They lie in the sand, trying not to movie.

Dare wince were three brothers, Carbine, Turbine, and Woodbine. Carbine woke in the Disturbed War, doubly clutching his thunder-mug; throwing his voice under the duress of a passing nursling, he shot weekly and sank into a comma. Turbine, blest by nun of his brother's talons, lay in white on both sighs of the robe, grinding his molecules. Woodbine was listed as missing in axioms. In a distant city, their mother wept. The Lord smiled at his Croatians. (They also Serb who all sustained in weight.)

The dark aegis and the sitting star of vampire. Old mind fields, raffles stacked in the reign, aircraft carrion, a beached wail. Does he still play the mandarin? He contemplates the ultimate pair o' ducks and mutters, Laquer my rare one.

Agassed at his whorable preposition, she waggled out of her skirt with a miniful look and a curt jester. He advanced his tremulous fallacy. She inverted her goblet. He swam the straits and narrows, she lewdly winnowed, he knocked at the door drooped in sea-weed, she bore wetness to the billowing dunderhead. He owled, she swal-lowed, they dissipated into thin heir. Absolute, my Absolute! she cried. At this instance he finely attained alignment like Sid Arthur, the loins lying at his feet, the lamps gambling in the meadow.

He love her so he give her some domineerings. Ho, ho, she cuckled.

There is the Cheap Executive and his staph, whose job is to execute. There is the Supreme Cart, dressed in black roads, whose job is to see the elocutions are perfectly lethal. There is Congress, mostly with secretaries. For the wrest, thugs, thieves, rubber barrens. They dream of going down on the anals of history.

The Cheap Executive comes on television, so to speak. His brows are knitted into a poison rug of ingratiating hatred. His hams clasp each udder as if frozen in strangle. A voice issues from the tomb of the thorax, full of reinsurance. No knead for panic. Not dead in vein. Business as usury. Public orifice. Offal sacrifice. Whirled leadershit.

Our farther, whose art is heavy, hollow bead I name. Die, kingpin, come; die, wheel, be dumb, inert as it is uneven. Gibbous this day airedaley bread, and fork over our test-passes as we fuck over them that test-pass against us. Elitist snot and a dumb nation and delirious primeval. For dyin' is the gingham and the flour and the gory, for rubber and rubber. Aye, men?

There were Patriark and Matriark and Baby Ark. Baby Ark was called Herman Aphrodite. S/he cried him/herself to sleep, sob-sister/brother, crying, Salmon's been leaping in *my* bed. S/he recede gargled messages. Something about a bottle of the sixes. Something about a menstrual show. Something about poker or poke her or polka, accordion to faminist teary. Men sauna in corporal guano, while galgirls decanter past on their white scallions, twirling their laureates, waving, Otiose, Omegas!

One light in the black, one young version, snowy, under things, made her bad now lye in it. But hoo that blackface in the widow-pain, hoo that burnt car kiss—ooh Black Panzer Man, out of site like a black star, and purr maid soddenly real eyes: she de spoils, she belittle pink booty—at the wonder now, the conk and the conqueror root. And he brake and anther, and he tariff her negli-gence, and he sock her nibbles with his furry tong and he dig his fungos in her squishy grass and he trickle her vassal and bobble her lobotomies till she summer salt and one swallow make him spring, and at lass she throned up bleached and grasping on his sable promontory. For all her nightmare come true and yet she love him yes she do, who plough deep in the agony and teeth shine in the nape and all that blood all over the Lord's white tidbit.

For years the Centaur had dreamed of election to the Cent. Now umpires of numbers tumble from his west pocket, a fifth a day, twists his skeleton key in the closets of Georgetown. Quick deals in cloaca-rooms, buttonhole, cornhole, secret saddest, best man at marriage of Lana the Free and Homo the Brave, never consomméd. Sum day a lad with bulging precepts and rackety legs will hand him a shoobox, saying, this is for you, Pa Drone. A waxy statute lies in the Rotunda, and the stern feces of the Four Fodders rankle in the gloom.

The Centaur's untensions were strychnine honorable, though she hoist her pedicles and bit him struck her fur thing, things rearly seen now a daisy. He only oysters on the bolster, sub-dude, lump, drooling Thigh Kingdom Come. With sudden ignition she screams

Majority Whip!—he shivs with pleasure. Free Enter Prize!—he fills
his pants. You know this Centaur. He like to incinerate that you are
his twin brothel.

I plunge my legions to the frog, the anointed snakes of Numerica,
and slithery public, the bitchy stands, one nation under guard,
invisible, with levity and justice for oil.

In the beginning was the beguine, which was gaud. Thus came
Jesus Crassus who foundered Chi Chi Chi and rose on the
Thursday. Thus came Macher Roger the beer typhoon, staggering
on the deck of Dollar Bill, king of demons and ace of space, who in
turn bestrides an enormous turdle of whom you may have hurdle.
Thus came Funny Money and Falsie Love and their only blubbered
son, His In a Sense. The Angle of Death plays the Angle of Mercy
—no contessa. God stands on their wings, trying to dismember his
lines. This is the muddle. There is no and.

SMALL SONG

Let Iddo praise the Lord with the Moth—the writings of man perish as the garment, but the Book of God endureth forever.

TO A MINOR POET
OF THE ANTHOLOGY

Where now is the memory of the days
that were your days on earth, that spun the thread
of luck and grief and were, for you, the world?

They were swept away in the measurable torrent
of years. You're a word in an index.

To others the gods gave everlasting laurel,
inscriptions on coins and obelisks, avid biographers;
of you, my obscure friend, we know only
that, one evening, you heard a nightingale.

Among the asphodel of the shades, your meager shade
will feel that the gods have been ungenerous.

But the days are a tangle of commonplace miseries,
and what better luck than to be the ash
of which oblivion is made?

On other heads the gods have poured
the relentless light of glory,
that peers into the hidden and picks out flaws,
glory, that ends by ruining the rose it adores—
to you, brother, they have shown themselves more merciful.

In the ecstasy of a dusk that will never be night,
you hear the voice of Theocritus' nightingale.

after Borges

THE FIELDS OF THE DEAD

I

Walking all afternoon the fields of the dead
I stopped where the grass flared thick
under an oak and leaned on a stone
to rest from the high sun.
I sat there cooling in my sweat,
tracing the worn lines, names and years
and the little graven images that harvest shadow.
The names near dazed me.
In the still air they seemed to rise
above the stone like heat waves,
and Solomon entered me
still mourning Abigail,
mourning Samuel, Jesse, John,
none of whom lasted a year,
and finally Iris, wife to Solomon, also mourning,
Gone But Not Forgotten.
Not quite yet.
All around, the small slabs sunken in the grass
and a few mansions, grey and innocent.
I felt a road running beneath where I lay.

Time. Buzzing of flies
in the silence.

Clouds piling up, sun almost down
and in its slant of light

I saw the slope
bursting with graves,
graves and evergreens and all the summer's greens,
even cut flowers breathed in a new light.
I rose from my grassy mound and walked a ways
into the freshening garden.

2

It is night.
I am standing outside the low stone wall of the kingdom,
an iron spike under my palm, dust
under my feet. Well, I can't help it,
it *is* dust, and I can't help pressing my hand against the point.
Looking for miles down the empty road,
streetlamps at intervals throwing brief pools on the darkness,
I can almost see to the end of my life,
almost beyond . . .

LOOKING INTO THE FIRE

The fire speaks.
Some logs cry out drily before they die,
others go up like San Lorenzo and that's it.
A band of crickets launches a wild harangue,
a beseeching wing,
a crazy music,
—my eyes get caught up
in the flames of the carnival—
wait, somebody's living in that wood!
The crowd shouts before disguising itself as ashes.

SMALL SONG

Someone lies down alone
In the arms of the new moon,
Someone I think I must know
If I had eyes to see.

What use to pretend we are free
While everything groans not so?
There are these wingless shoulder blades,
These heavy feet on the earth.

ON THE BURNING COAST

to which he comes as often as he can
grandmother sits
waiting for him with thin hands

hands that over eighty years
grasped at everything
slowly folding into a final sculpture

she has forgotten
the sacred embroidery the country dances
even the prayers intended for these moments
her dead husband
everything
all she has is a few dollars
for the fee

evening mingles tenderly with the horizon
putting out all fire

it's like a fairy tale she says
isn't it Alex

and hobbles off across the beach
to join the misty figure
who stands knee-deep in the breaking surf

FOUR-PART PSALM

I

All phantoms of the day
Nothing burns or pierces this dense fog
Ghost of the table
Ghost of the typewriter
Past and future mutilate the appetite

2

I have my name
For the whole shambling charade
Enter and exit
Tentative changeling imperious swineherd morning

3

Nothing expounds
Father and motherandchild
Vestures of empty space swaying here or there
Time sits high
On a throne of calcium

4

Debris of the void
Debut of the blind dancer
We too

Blind dancely hands outstretched
Even as the door opens
A little wind
Even as the oak
All its arms lifting cups of light to the zenith

TWILIGHT UNDER PINE RIDGE

Earth between two lights,
one just now draining away
from tiny trees on the western shoulder,
and one to come,
as the stars begin to open in the field of night.
On every slope great trees are flowering
in beautiful relation and yet
all solitary. In the early darkness
clear voices leave off
and fold inward toward sleep.
The grass
parts.
Lord God slides forward on his belly.

GOOD FORTUNE
BY BLACK MOUNTAIN

Late night full moon
black mountain rising pale and massy
the congregation of the trees
share their silver bread

most stars have hidden themselves in moonlight
a few stand shy
like children on some lonely farm

black mountain
one could sleep in its shadow
one could sleep on its full breast
and wake in the milky night
happy

and these rocks
glowing like phosphorus of another planet

they have made you a rich man

TO BE A GIANT

Hard, hard
to be a giant,
especially here
where there are few
and one goes crazy.
Should he catch a glimpse
of the little people
running in the fields below,
their hats falling off,
it is all he can do
to keep from crying.
On white hot days
he wanders the hills
of yellow grass,
eating saplings
and stray calves,
ignoring the pains
in his belly. He carries
a small pocket mirror
in which he sometimes
looks at pieces
of his enormous face
and sometimes holds it out,
flashing the commandments of the sun
to the empty hills.

LAST DAYS IN SALT LAKE CITY

Dwarfed by a building that would have delighted Mussolini,
A blonde shape hardens in the bright mist.

It's the Angel Moroni, resplendent in gold drag,
Calling the faithful to shop at the Company Store.

Faces heavy as concrete, catatonic faces,
The lost tribe, getting more and more lost.

The radio says make Jesus your business partner
At 10% and the Christ can suck hind titty.

I came here to muse on a bone in the Jewish graveyard,
And the banks locked arms with their cousins the mausoleums.

And the last malcontent poet to pass this way
Was detained in front of the wall of a firing squad.

Did you hear that, feet? I won't think less of you
If you leap to a hasty conclusion and split for the coast.

UNSENT LETTER TO LUIS SALINAS

It's hot in the mountains now even at night,
and soon you will be in Texas
sweating the sun and looking for the virgin in Mexican bars.
Obsidian eyes that see the human
and the inhuman with the same anguish,
hands of broken wheat,
bones worn down to frail shadows,
all the weariness of the poor
burns clearly through raw alcohol.
I picture you pushing a heavy brown breast to your mouth
as if you could get away for just one night
or even twenty minutes.
Stay with her, brother, laughing
and showing your bad teeth—
while you slept
they stole your country again
and while they steal
the bed creaks with the weight of the whole world.
May you have many children
and the gringos none.

THE SILENCE

How many times God will remember
the silence of the beginning,
that silence which even God himself couldn't endure,
which was finally to blame for our being here now—
he lost his head, and clawing at the earth picked up some
        mud and made us.

And thus ended the silence,
and then began the howling,
interrupted now and then by a faint twittering
when we make love in our sleep.

ONE OF YOU

There are some men who have deserted life,
who finally couldn't stand the taste
and spit it out. Something in them is broken
in such a way that only death can heal it,
or worse.
          Sometimes you see one in a Mexican village,
walking aimlessly, regarding creation
with a slack stare, while all around him sit
the small dark inhabitants of the place,
taut bellies, eaters of suffering. One night
he walks for hours, out past the lighted doorways
and faint snatches of incomprehensible speech
to where the darkness is total and the life
he wanted to remember breathes in the grass
which he can't see. He gets down on his knees
and weeps a little and on his hands
and loses it and finally falls asleep.

In the morning he will order breakfast, hands
curled on the spotless linen, dry face
facing the empty sunlight—but it's the meal
after the last and you will not recognize him.
He is back, and he is one of you again.

TRYING TO BEGIN

Here you are once more, sitting at a table,
hands folded and ankles crossed, the most
ordinary of mornings and absolutely nothing to do.
And slowly, neither awake nor asleep,
you start to feel
you must have been lost a long time in the cells of paper,
a faint tinkle of dust
coming back to life in the world of the ear.
The coffee is cold,
yet always the same white ground and the same ghostly figures
weaving toward a distant light,
and lines groping for some opening in the crushed wall,
and lines that glisten like the snail's whereabouts
down to this wet sheaf
that might have just arrived, so heavy and fresh,
from wheat farmers in regions of ice and cloud.
Or maybe just a layer of sodden leaves
left on the doorstep by the nightlong rain.

THE STREAM FLOWING

I remember the creek that ran beside the golf course,
slow and black over rocks; patches of snow;
withies of willow streaming out in the wind,
born to it and, I imagine, bowing and scraping.

I would sometimes sit there shivering and looking out
at the flagless frostbitten greens, the naked trees
that bordered the bleak fairways and a sky
the ashen color of longing and disappointment.

Early winter, it was. And then I remember
the girl I brought there one night—the summer after?
We lay deep on the grassy bank, almost hidden,
and I touched her warm secret hair for the first time.

I can still hear the sound of water pushing by us,
the sound of her breath in my ear as I touched her there,
my stiff boyish hand trembling against her belly.
Her name was June. I could feel a pulse where I touched.

There were little lights in the breathing darkness around us.
Her eyes were closed and I was looking past her
at nameless summer stars and pulsing fireflies
and what must have been houses far off in the night somewhere.

Nothing else happened there. We were afraid,
and lay in the matted crush of the maidenhair

and chilly rivergrass. We could smell the night
and see the willow cascading over our heads.

I remember the last time I went there, alone and older,
three or four winters later. The clear water
was still flowing, now between snow-covered banks
and white fields stretched away to the hem of the sky.

One day melts into another and into years,
twenty years that flowed on and lost themselves in the sea.
Where is June, and the boy that she held to her body
on that bank once? Well, useless to think of her now,

and useless to think of the boy, by now a man—
each with a husband or wife, in a house far off
in the midst of another life, where I remember
the fern verging that stream and the stream flowing.

AN OLD STORY

1

We met at the edge of the city
Where the road heaps its dust and ends dead
And we kept house.

We kept it in two transparent solitudes,
In two vials of alcohol,
In two lockets—

In one, beheaded geese run to the creamery.
In the other, your farm tilts into the sea
And I cannot find you.

I find you where I found you before,
On the hill of the dead,
Under the shadow of the oak

Whose leaves were sacred once.

2

Once we were horses standing in cold grass
Side by side, head to tail,
Barely touching . . .

You know how horses do.
Now we're just people, wondering
Where it went.

Walking in graveyards,
Two or three graves apart,
Or on the bottom of the sea.

3

Let me begin again.

Under mulberries, in late summer,
The three of us sat to look at the full moon
And mountains steeped in moonlight.

Looking, I thought I should live forever
And love you at least that long.
I was wrong.

He, the third person, was our friend
The moon. Light faded on his mouth,
His eyes refilled with darkness.

He's shining again. And we're still here,
Straining against the ropes
As the whiteness spreads in our hair . . .

BEFORE AND AFTER LOVE

Neither the intimacy of your face, both young and old,
nor the openings of your body, still mysterious, still girlish
          and eager,
nor the daily happenings of your life, your speech or silence,
can be as unfathomable a gift
as to gaze upon your body evenly breathing
in the grateful night of my arms.
Virgin once more, miraculously, through the absolving
          power of sleep,
voluptuous and pure as a happiness memory chooses,
grant me that outskirt of your life that you yourself do not
          possess.
Perhaps, in my wakefulness,
I will make out the farthest shore of your being
and I will see you for the first time, perhaps,
as God must see,
beyond the smoke of Time's illusions,
apart from love,
apart from me.

                                   after Borges

N. W.

On a certain street there is a certain door,
Unyielding, around which rockroses rise,
Charged with the scent of a lost paradise,
Which in the evening sunlight opens no more,
Or not to me. Once, in a better light,
Dearly awaited arms would wait for me
And in the impatient fading of the day
The joy and peace of the embracing night.
No more of that. Now, a day breaks and dies,
Releasing empty hours, and impure
Fantasies, and the abuse of literature,
The lawless images and artful lies,
And pointless tears, and envy of other men.
And then the longing for oblivion.

after Borges

ILL LIT BLUES

The lights come on so early on these winter afternoons;
The darkness creeps up early, winter afternoons,
And somewhere a piano is picking out a musty tune.

With less than an explanation you have taken your liberty
And arranged without thinking that nobody else but me
Will be sitting here in the dark like a granite effigy.

Well, no use complaining, there are a million people like me,
And everything as usual is exactly what it must be:
Character is fate, they say—I'm sure that you agree.

And they say love is easy as the turning of a page—
Haven't you heard that, honey?—like the turning of a page?
But they mumble something different in the back rooms of old age.

I'm not a first-time loser, I've been down this road before,
And once again I find myself standing outside a door;
But even as I spell it out, I still don't know the score.

Yet the truth is plain as day, love, all you need do is look;
I can see it clear as daylight, saw it in your parting look—
Love is a sudden emptiness like the closing of a book.

A WAY OF SAYING GOODBYE

At last the theater darkens. Nobody's here.
The old whore begins to look young and sexy again,
and the lies that were told, the lies and the sighs lean
out of the balconies, out of the memory of the air.

Wanting to put your finger on the truth,
you lay down beside her awhile, not sure who
but hopeful that in that dark there were two of you,
that you might touch the body and feel its breath—

or else you thought you did, which is not the same thing.
A mist hangs in what little light remains alive,
like the fumes of a drug, the burning up of a leaf,
the inaudible music that accompanies a dead song.

WORDS

We thought a day and a night of steady rain
Was plenty, but it's falling again, downright tireless.
I like it well enough, the mild crackle
In the alleyway, lulling or minatory, either way
Full of the freshness of life. Much like words.
But words don't fall exactly; they hang there
In the heaven of language, immune to gravity
If not to time, entering your mind
From no direction, traveling no distance at all,
And with rainy persistence tease from the spread earth
So many ravishing scents. And they recur,
Delicious to nose and tongue. The word cunt
Often recurs, the word more than the thing,
Perhaps because I came to it so late.
Ocean recurs, perhaps for the same reason, and egg,
Horseman and horse manure, bridal, sap,
And lap with its childish and charming delight in rhyme,
And denial describes its orbit, and blight, and transfigure.
And though I'd argue that those smells of earth
Under the rain's long kneading hands are sweeter
And more ambiguous than any words,
Darkness, one word that does seem to fall,
Falls, and we're back where we started from.

MERCY

for Olivia and Peter

In an orgy of silence the moon rose
And we sat looking up. Then the wind
Swaying the flowers with a gentle force
Broke open its sweetness on our foreheads.

She said a word long since forgotten,
And you listened to the beating of your heart,
And just over the mountain one white cloud
Came lordly in the radiance of the night.

Something always escapes us, but then the air
Was a drug that we three blindly inhaled,
Till we were lost to hunger and suffering
And could not but behold and be beholden.

Mercy, she said. Now I remember.
And we sat quiet, under a listening sky.
For a moment it seemed we held it all in our hands,
Then let it go, and that was the best of all.

OF THE POWER OF THOUGHT

The rain falls like an army, clattering
on the thin plastic tied to four trees
for a flimsy roof, though not to be despised.
We watch the drenched pines through a veil of water
and wait, feeling left out, as it gets dark.
It rains hard all evening, we can hear it
even over the hiss and crash of the river.
Curled like a toad in my clammy bag I wish
I was home, at my desk,
dry clothes, pen, paper,
old typewriter under the warm lamplight—
and here I am.

INTERLUDE: CLERIHEWS AND OTHER SPORTS

CLERIHEWS

Edmund Clerihew Bentley
Was literary, evidently,
But his chief claim to fame
Is his middle name.

William Makepeace Thackeray
Would have adored a frozen daiquiri,
But swallowed down his gin
Without dwelling on what might have been.

Oscar Wilde
Was most unjustly reviled:
Merely for loving his neighbor
He got two years' hard labor.

John Keats
Was not one of the Beats:
His habits were neater
And he wrote in meter.

Johann Sebastian Bach
At 2 a.m. sighed, "Ach,
Bring me some coffee, I gotta
Finish a cantata."

Johann Sebastian Bach
Was heard to murmur, "Ach,

If only I had a Moog,
I'd make short work of this fugue."

Arthur Hugh Clough
Wrote a lot of stuff,
But whether it was any good at all
I can't recall.

Mary Baker Eddy
Liked to put on a teddy
And try to engage her Savior
In the most ungodly behavior.

Edgar Allen Poe
I would rank very low;
I simply cannot bear
His dank tarns and hyacinth hair.

Percy Bysshe Shelley
Had more on his mind than his belly.
One can only take pity on
The author of *Epipsychidion.*

Edna St. Vincent Millay
In her brisk yet casual way
Took Bunny Wilson to bed.
Or so he said.

In public, Robert Browning
Was never seen frowning.
Let me be very emphatic:
He usually looked ecstatic.

John Dryden
Never looked for a hole to hide in.
Did he run away from MacFlecknoe?
Heck, no.

Allen Tate
Was a victim of fate;
But let it be said,
So were the Confederate dead.

EUROCENTRIC RAG

I make a lot of money and I have a perfect tan;
I wear Armani clothing, I'm a very fancy Dan;
I've dominated women ever since the world began—
Yes, I'm phallocentric, logocentric, Eurocentric Man!

Oppression is my favorite sport, I play it with élan,
And I scorn the weak and womanish, the sloth, the also-ran;
Let them forage for their dinner in my silver garbage can
And thank their generous benefactor, Eurocentric Man.

I've conquered everybody from Peru to Hindustan
And I make 'em speak my language, though they very rarely can;
I'm the king, the pope, the CEO, the chieftain of the clan—
Yes, I'm phallologo, logophallo, Eurocentric Man!

The beauty with the hothouse grapes, the young boy with the fan
Are only minor luxuries, like my Silver Cloud sedan;
I bet you're very curious about my Master Plan.
I sit and pare my fingernails. I'm Eurocentric, man.

TAILGATERS

Something there is that doesn't love a wall
But passionately adores a shopping mall.

Of man's first disobedience and the fruit
Comes apple brandy and the three-piece suit.

"O World, I cannot hold thee close enough!"
Edna stage-whispered, and the world said, "Tough."

Euclid alone has looked on Beauty bare;
The rest of us must see it covered with hair.

They flee from me that sometime did me seek.
Could be your new deodorant's too weak.

Thou still unravished bride of quietness,
Thou foster-child—come, give thy Dad a kiss.

I celebrate myself, and sing myself,
And gaze upon my photos on the shelf.

I think continually of the truly great,
And every now and then of the second-rate.

GREETINGS

1

Although my voice pretends that I am here,
I could be anywhere. You have my ear,
Which might not be around, but, then, it might.
My mind is absent too, but that's all right—
We'll reassemble presently, unpack,
Play all your messages and call you back.

2

The inmate is not in, or, let us say,
He's in the middle of his working day,
Or, as the case may be, his working night;
He is, for now, the sleepless eremite.
Here comes the little beep—you know the game:
Speak clearly, leave your number and your name.

3

I am asleep, or maybe only blotto;
I'm reading books or out running around—
In any case, I'm incommunicado.
This newfangled device will hold your sound
Till I get home or in the mood to hear it,
So talk to me—I'm listening in spirit.

GLOSSES AND VARIATIONS

HER SPARROW

Wear black, you Venuses and you Cupids,
you lucky lovers and ladies' men.
My darling's sparrow is dead,—pet sparrow
who was my darling's sweetest pleasure,
whom she loved better than her own eyes;
he was her honey, he was closer to her
than a young girl to her own mother;
nor would he stray from her lap or bosom
but hopping about, now here, now there,
piped his tune only to her his mistress.
And now he goes the shadow-brimmed road
from which, they say, no traveler returns.
Damn you, damn you, shadows of Orcus,
indifferent shadows that swallow all beauty:
you have stolen away a beautiful sparrow.
So cruel, so cruel! Ah, poor little sparrow!
Look what you've done now—my darling's eyes
red and swollen, swimming with tears.

after Catullus

JERRY'S STRETCH

What's Jerry doing? up all night scratching an itch
With his mom and his sis, their clothes scattered every which way?
And giving his own uncle horns—how could he do it?
Can you even imagine how low he has sunk in sin?
A stain so indelible, not all the incestuous gods,
Not even Ocean, could ever wash it away.
How could he sink any lower? —Unless, perhaps,
He could get his head low enough . . .

after Catullus

ALL IN THE FAMILY

Jerry's lost weight—and why not? Have you seen his mother?
Such a lively performer at her age, so pretty, so giving—
And his succulent sister? and uncle, a man who, like mother,
Just can't say no? And girls, girls by the dozen,
All kissing cousins—when does he eat and sleep?
Well, even if he cut back, kept it all in the family,
Touched only what mustn't be touched—he'd still be thin.

after Catullus

ANCIENT EPIGRAMS

Stella, high-priced whore whose breath is the scent of money,
whose mouth and loins have set whole towns on fire—
I did her, naked and wanton, again and again
until day broke and my dream ended; and it cost nothing.

Never again will I go down on my knees
before her barbarous beauty, never again
burn in my bed alone: in blissful sleep
I will do whatever I please with her—it will cost nothing.

after an anonymous poet

Stranger, go tell the citizens of Sparta:
We lie here still obedient to their orders.

after Simonides

Word of your death.

I shed tears, and I remembered
the many times we talked the moon down the sky.

Henri C., secret agent of Pasadena,
once my friend, now vacant dust,

your songs of intelligence
elude the grasp of the inquisitive gods

after Kallimachos

Only in body was this girl a slave,
And now it too finds freedom in the grave.

after Damaskios

What do you like to do when you're drunk in bed?
The same as when you're sober, dear—give head.

after Martial

They say there are nine Muses: count again.
Remember Sappho of Lesbos? That makes ten.

after Plato

TWO VERSIONS OF THE EMPEROR'S EPIGRAM

My little charmer, wayward little soul,
Guest and companion of this flesh and bone,
Where are you off to, irretrievably,
Pale naked little thing, mute and alone,
And not so merry as you used to be?

Little charmer, wandering little soul,
House guest and companion of this body,
Where are you off to now, and at whose call,
Poor naked little creature, stiff and pale,
You who were once so witty, life of the party?

after Hadrian

MY STARS

On the day I was born,
The unalterable stars altered.
If I decided to sell lamps,
It wouldn't get dark till the day I died.

Some stars. Whatever I do,
I'm a failure before I begin.
If I suddenly decided to sell shrouds,
People would suddenly stop dying.

after Abraham ibn Ezra

JERUSALEM

Beautiful heights, city of a great King,
From the western coast my desire burns towards thee.
Pity and tenderness burst in me, remembering
Thy former glories, thy temple now broken stones.
I wish I could fly to thee on the wings of an eagle
And mingle my tears with thy dust.
I have sought thee, love, though the King is not there
And instead of Gilead's balm, snakes and scorpions.
Let me fall on thy broken stones and tenderly kiss them—
The taste of thy dust will be sweeter than honey to me.

after Halevi

GRAVES

And where are the graves, so many graves
Of all who have died on the earth since the beginning?
Grave tunneling into grave,
Headstone and obelisk crumbled into one dust,
Bodies heaped upon bodies, in motionless orgy—
All sleeping together in bottomless holes,
Fragments of chalk,
Stained rubies.

after Moses ibn Ezra

ON HER PORTRAIT

This that you see, this colorful pretense
That makes a show of what its skill can do
(The colors proving none of it is true)
Is nothing but the subtlest fraudulence;
This ornament by which flattery has done
All that it could to cover up time's smears,
To overcome the horrors of the years
And conquer old age and oblivion,

Is the empty trappings of anxiety,
An airy flower under the wind's weight,
A ludicrous protection against fate,
A stupid business, a lost fantasy,
A withered appetite, then, even less:
A corpse—dead flesh—dust—shadow—nothingness.

after Sor Juana

LAMENT FOR JONATHAN

Must even princes bow down to the hour?
Must they too fade like base things, even the hand
that sealed the fate of others, even the power
that stamped itself on the submissive land?

But you, the opening letter of your heart,
the sun that warmed my face, how could you then
suddenly disappear? I have no art
to bring you back. If only one were here
whose shining seed might father you again!

A shadowy hand has come between us twain—
and he who loved you lives as in a dream
and must not blanch to hear that you are slain.
Like beasts rubbed raw that swallow back their pain
I want to crawl away somewhere and scream.

From my most private places everywhere
you have been ripped from me, like the fine hair
under my arms, or the luxurious curls,
the pleasure garden frequented by girls

before you drew all my confusions clear,
as one unties a knot—if knots were men.
Once I raised my eyes and there you were.
But I will never see your face again.

after Rilke

DAVID SINGS BEFORE SAUL

Do you not hear it, Sire, my instrument
fling outward the deep space of our wandering
where stars swim near us, all uncomprehending,
until at last we're here, like rain descending,
and what a flowering follows that descent!

Girls you still had the power to bend and enter
flower into women who melt down my defenses;
fragrance of virgins drifts upon your senses;
and young boys nearby somewhere, young and slender,
breathing intensely, the dark air charged with glances.

Ah that my strings might bring them crowding back,
the blazing nights of love, insomniac,
those lithe bodies pleasuring and pleasured
(grown heavier since spread for your attack)—
but the tune's gone reeling, drunken and unmeasured.

I can sense your memories, Lord, of that old splendor,
would pluck its music— But how is one to render
the ecstatic cries and groans of the young and slender?

after Rilke

THE GRAVE

in memory of those fallen in the Ukraine

There are many like him here, without epitaph, without a mound.
The ox pulling a plough stumbles upon him,
The peasant behind the plough, furious, curses him,
And his clearing will be the shelter of the locust.

The field, before autumn—and only a cloud weeps for him
With cold cries. A storm silences it;
And thus he is mourned. No one to say Kaddish.
The path bends around him and does not cry, O father!

Even this year, look, his land is becoming green,
Awakening from sleep and turning its burned face,
Aftergrowth bursting up from everywhere,
And the stalks of wheat mock him with sighing and scraping.

And this fellow, struck down by fire, decaying in soot and slime,
He doesn't know why the spade dug him a furrow,
Nor why he lived his life of pain and sorrow,
Nor why he was cut down and thrown here before his time.

after Tchernichovsky

JULIO CAMPAL

We were walking to your funeral, eleven friends.
And the twenty-eight letters of your alphabet,
your letters, Julio, all set loose,
all of which once went willingly in bonds.

Throw letters up into the air, like dice:
always they will come down to earth a poem.
Sow the scattered, fragmentary bones
in this lot or that lot
or in the most remote:
they will be gathered and made whole again, down
to the least fingerbone.

Twenty-eight letters, Julio Campal.
And your secret hidden forever behind their veil.

after Gerardo Diego

TO THE LIKENESS OF A CAPTAIN
IN CROMWELL'S ARMIES

Even the walls of Mars would not impress
This captain, whom the Lord's word fortifies;
From another light, another age, his eyes,
That have looked out on slaughter, look at us.
On the sword's hilt the hand just now alighting;
The war moves through a countryside of green;
Beyond the dark smoke England can be seen,
Horses and glory and your day of fighting.
Ambition and desire, captain, are snares:
Vain is your armor, vain the pride and power
Of man, whose whole existence is an hour;
All of this has been over now for years.
The steel destined to wound you has turned to rust,
And you are now among the damned, like us.

after Borges

BALLAD OF THE STRANGER

The story is always the same story,
With every step retraced;
They tell the story in Silver City
And in Tombstone to the west.

There are always two that they talk of—
A stranger and a local guy.
It is always evening. The evening star
Shines in the evening sky.

They have never seen each other's faces
Nor will they ever again;
The quarrel is not about money
Or what women do for men.

The stranger has heard tell of a man
Whose courage has won renown.
Now he has come to see for himself,
And searches all over town.

He asks him nicely to step outside
In a quiet, unthreatening voice:
They both know, and neither would wish
To bring shame on the house.

Now two hands go to their holsters—
Each suddenly fires a round.

Now a man lies still in the street
Without having made a sound.

They never met before that evening.
They will not meet again.
It was not greed that started it
Nor passion for a woman.

No use in being more skillful,
No use in being more fit;
Always the one who dies is the one
Who went out looking for it.

All their lives the two men
Were living for that test.
Time has already erased their faces—
Soon, their names erased.

after Borges

EINAR TAMBARSKELVER

(Heimskringla, I, 117)

Odin or red Thor or the White Christ . . .
They matter little, the names, the gods behind them;
There is no other duty than to be brave,
And Einar, leathery captain of men, was that.
He was foremost among the Norwegian archers
And expert in the handling of the sword,
Of ships and men. Of his trajectory
Through time, there now remains to us one sentence,
Which gives off light in the chrestomathies.
He said it in the din of a sea battle.
The lost day's fighting done, the starboard side
Open to boarding, a last shot snapped his bow.
The king asked him what was that that had broken
Behind his back and Einar Tambarskelver
Replied, *Norway, my Lord, between your fingers.*
Centuries later, someone saved the story
In Iceland. And I now transcribe it here,
So distant from those oceans, from that spirit.

after Borges

JOHNNY RAFTERY

Montana somewhere, 1890 or so—
My father crossed paths with him. Perhaps they exchanged
A few sparing and long-forgotten words.
He remembered nothing of the man but this:
The back of his dark-skinned left hand crisscrossed
With scratches—claw marks. Back then, on the ranch,
Everyone lived out his own destiny:
This guy broke horses, that one was a wrangler,
Another man could rope like nobody else—
It fell to Raftery to hunt down cougars.
Whenever a cougar preyed upon the sheepfold
Or someone heard her screaming in the darkness,
Raftery would track her into the bush.
He took a knife with him and a few dogs.
And when at last he closed with her in a thicket
He would set the dogs on her. The tawny beast
As like as not sprang suddenly on the man
Who shook a jacket wrapped around his arm,
Both shield and an incitement. The white belly
Was unprotected and the animal
Felt the steel entering her until she died.
The pain was fated, yes, and infinite.
He went on killing always the same cougar
Which was immortal. Don't let this surprise you
Too much. His destiny is yours, and mine,
Except for the fact that *our* cougar takes forms
That change continuously. Call it Chance,
Or Love, or Hatred,—call it Every Moment.

after Borges

THE GOLEM

If (as the Greek asserts in his *Cratylus*)
A thing's name is the archetype of the thing,
Then, from the letters of *rose* all roses spring
And from the word *Nile* the length of the Nile arises.

And, made entirely of consonants and vowels,
There must be a dread, unspeakable Name, the essence
Of God encoded, which Omnipotence
Guards in its secret letters and syllables.

Adam knew it and so did the stars over Eden,
But afterwards (or so the cabalists say)
The corrosion of sin wiped it utterly away
And from the generations it was therefore hidden.

Of the ingenuity and innocence of men
There is no end. We know there was a time
When the people chosen of God sought for the Name—
Long the night watches in the ghettos then.

Unlike those who worm their mist and fog
Into the mists and fogs of history,
Still green and living is the memory
Of Judah the Lion, who was a rabbi in Prague.

Thirsting to know what is known to Deity,
Judah lost himself in the permutations
Of letters, the endless intricate variations,
And at last pronounced the Name, which is the Key,

The Portal, the Echo, the Host, the Sacred Place,
Over an inert clay figure which he kneaded
With stiff hands, patiently trying to feed it
The secrets of Letters, the secrets of Time and Space.

This earthen semblance raised its drowsy eyelids
And saw, for the first time, forms and colors,
Which made no sense, drowned as they were in murmurs,
And tried to move a little, clumsy and timid.

Gradually he saw that he was (like us, his brothers)
A prisoner in this vast and sonorous net
Of Earlier, Later, Yesterday, Now, Not Yet,
Right and Left, You and I, those Others.

(The cabalist who played creating deity
Dubbed this enormous creature of his the Golem;
This is one of the facts that Gershom Scholem
Relates to us somewhere in his learned study.)

The rabbi expounded to him the universe—
This is my foot; this is yours; this is string—
Until, after many years, the grotesque thing
Was able to sweep out the synagogue, more or less.

Perhaps in the tracing of letters there was some mistake,
Or in the pronouncing of the sacred Name;
For all the sorcery and the lofty aim,
The apprentice man could not even learn to speak.

His eyes, less those of a man than of a dog,
And even less of a dog than of a thing,

Followed the rabbi through the wavering
Half-light of the cell of the synagogue.

There must have been something unearthly in the Golem,
Seeing that at his footsteps the rabbi's cat
Ran and hid. (This cat is not in Scholem,
But across the centuries, I intuit it.)

Raising to God his creaturely hands, all thumbs,
He aped the rabbi at his rapt devotions,
Or smiling stupidly, he took a notion
To bow down low in ludicrous salaams.

The rabbi gazed on him with tender affection
And not a little horror. *How* (he wondered)
Could I this pitiful child have engendered,
Leaving behind the wisdom of inaction?

Why did I think to add one symbol more
To the infinite series? Why did I give to the skein
That winds and unwinds eternally and in vain
Another cause and effect, another care?

It was at the end of this anguished monologue,
In the hour of hazy light, that he looked at his son.
Who will tell us what God felt, looking down
At *His* son, Judah the Lion, rabbi of Prague?

after Borges

PARIS, 1856

His long prostration has accustomed him
To reckoning on death. He'd be afraid
To go down to the strident day outside
And be among men. Stricken in life and limb,
Heinrich Heine fixes his thought anew
On time's river that floats him slowly away
From the half-darkness and harsh destiny
Of being a human being and a Jew.
He muses on the delicate melodies
Whose instrument he was, but well he knows
His music comes not out of birds or boughs
But out of time and its phantasmal days.
They will not save you, no, neither your flowers
Nor nightingales nor golden midnight hours.

after Borges

TO A FORGOTTEN POET OF 1935

To leave behind a verse for that sad hour
That watches us at day's edge, lying in wait;
To affix your signature to its grievous date
Of gold and shadow—that was your desire.
With what passion, as twilight deepened, you
Would toil over the peculiar verse
That till the extinction of the universe
Would manifest that hour's peculiar blue!
I don't know if you ever managed it,
My ghostly brother, or if you existed even,
But I am lonesome, and I wish oblivion
Could give back to the days your delicate
Shadow, that it might live in this worn shell
Of words in which the blues of evening dwell.

after Borges

A ROSE AND MILTON

Of roses in their infinite blossomings
That have been lost to time in time's abyss,
I want one to be spared from nothingness,
One without stain or sign among the things
That once existed. Fate grants me the grace,
The honor of first naming that sublime
And wordless flower, the rose that one last time
John Milton held a hairs-breadth from his face,
Not seeing it. From gardens long disperse,
O thou, yellow or white or burning red,
Come as by magic from thy myriad
Lost centuries and flourish in this verse,
Ivory, gold, or blood, or vague shadows
As in his hand once, O invisible rose.

after Borges

NOT SO SIMPLE

It's not all so simple in the yards of houses;
Floor after floor, the windows stare into space.
On cracked pavements, on bare, faded walls,
Every passing hour has left its trace.

It's not all so simple, how mirrors look at a room,
And there's something to read in the way the bookcase stands.
The heavy drapes, the carefully made bed
Are sinking down under the yoke of thought.

In every house there are many dark stairs.
Silent creatures come down them every morning
And go up every evening and close their doors.
I pray for them . . .

after Shin Shalom

THE MEANING OF SOUP

The meaning of soup has been lost.
                              —*A. Gide*

Life moves slowly, with a warm, oozing tread;
it smells like river mud, like cows and slow earth.
The woman under a man knows that smell.

An odor as nourishing as good soup,
a nutritious weeping, a few patient days . . .
(Here's where we eat, drink, breathe, and make love.)

Must I explain? Is there anyone who doesn't know this?
Life is a heavy humus, sweet and black.
It has the heat of the loins and insists on shedding tears.

It's the dammed-up river of the woman we love,
the ripe fruit of exhausted hours,
and a job, a house, an impulse, a routine.

Because all of us live and life is just like that.
It's not love, or happiness, or ideas, or the future.
It's just a hot, thick, dirty soup.

after Gabriel Celaya

REQUIEM

Manuel del Río, born
in Spain, died Saturday
the 11th of May, the result
of an accident. The body
is laid out at the D'Agostino
Funeral Home. Haskell. New Jersey.
There will be a sung Mass
at 9:30, in St. Francis.

It is a story that opens
in sunlight and stone, and ends
on a table, in D'Agostino's,
among flowers and electric candles.
It is a story that opens
on one shore of the Atlantic,
continues in a third-
class cabin over the waves
—or is it over the clouds?—
of those lost continents
sunk long before Plato,
and comes to an end in America
with a tow truck and a clinic,
a death notice and a sung Mass
in the church of St. Francis.

In the long run it makes no difference
where we die. Whether it smells
of rosemary or is carved out of stone

or snow or soaked in gasoline
—and whether a body turns into stone,
gasoline, snow, or just a smell—
what difference does it make?
The misery's not in dying
here, there, or somewhere else . . .

Requiem æternam,
Manuel del Río. Over the slab
in D'Agostino's the bulls of Spain
are grazing, Manuel, and there are flowers
(second-class funeral, coffin
smelling of winter fir),
which cost forty bucks. And they have stuck
some artificial ones
in with the ones picked
from the garden . . . *Libera me Domine*
de morte æterna . . . When a James dies,
or a Jacob, he will stare
at these same flowers, compliments
of Giulio or Manuel . . .

Now down to the crest of your life
eagle talons. *Dies iræ.*
The misery's not in dying
Dies illa here or there,
but so ingloriously . . .

Your fathers
swelled the entire earth

with the seed of their daring.
When a Spaniard fell down dead
a wound opened in the cosmos.
Not in D'Agostino's Funeral Home
did they keep their deathwatches
but by campfires, in the midst
of their horses and weapons. Heroes,
always. Statues, with the faces
obliterated. Yet decked out
in the old parrot colors, the colors
of power and imagination.

He did not die that way. He did not die
for any beautiful madness.
(For a long time now Spaniards have died
anonymous and prudent
or else in some stupid madness
between brothers: whenever you slash
a wineskin, your brother's blood spurts out.)
He came one day to this place
because his country is poor. The world
Libera me Domine is the homeland.
And he died. Having founded no city,
having given his name to no ocean.
All he did was die for seventeen
bucks (which he'd translate
into pesetas). *Requiem æternam.*
And now in D'Agostino's they visit him,
Poles, Irish,

Spaniards, those who died
over the weekend.

Requiem æternam.
It is really over.
Finished. The body
lies in D'Agostino's
Funeral Home. Haskell. New Jersey.
There will be a sung Mass
for his soul.

I have confined myself here
to thinking about an obituary clipped
from a New York newspaper.
Objectively. Without flying off
into verse. Objectively.
A Spaniard like millions
of Spaniards. And I have said
nothing to anyone
about being on the verge of tears.

after José Hierro

ODYSSEUS

And returning at last to his birthplace he found the ocean
and various fish and seaweed gliding on the slow waves.
A sun weakening on the hem of the sky.

Error forever recurs, thought Odysseus, sick at heart,
as he made his way to the crossroads near the city
to look for the road to a birthplace that was not water.

A wanderer, a man exhausted by dreams and longings,
among people who spoke some other Greek—
the words he had stored for provision had meanwhile gone bad.

For a moment he imagined he had slept a long time
and come back to people who were not surprised to see him,
whose eyes regarded him blankly.

He questioned them with his hands and they tried to understand,
from a distance.
The crimson was fading, darkening, on the hem of that sky.

At last they took hold of the children who had gathered around him
and led them away.
And light after light glowed yellow in house after house.

Dew came then and touched him on the forehead.
Came wind and kissed him on the lips.
Came water and washed his feet, like the old nurse,
and did not notice the scar
and went running on down the slope, as water will.

after Chaim Guri

I SAW

I saw a white bird disappear in the black night
and I knew it wouldn't be long for the light
of my eyes in that same night.

I saw a cloud as small as a man's hand
and I knew, though the first ripples widen in the pond,
that I haven't been able to make anyone understand.

I saw a leaf that fell, a leaf is falling.
Time is short. I am not complaining.

after Natan Zach

GAUGUIN

His journalist father
wrote some remarkable articles
liberty—he said—
is the dignity of the people
notwithstanding
he died on his way to Lima
where Paul would turn eleven
one morning—11:15—
June
    1859

later
deck hand on a merchantman
he discovered the smells
seasonings mists of Brittany
he would always love
the vast stretch of low tide
                that moment
when the retreat of the sea
seems to carry off
our shadowy ills
        abstract rage

but still
he served in the ranks of that army
that had no way of stopping
the Prussian advance
          —Bismarck remarked

that the French soldier was a coward
and as lightweight as his underwear—

                            knowing nothing
of utopian socialism
perhaps he would think of his father

                      when
Thiers' army was emptying its rifles
into the editors of the Official Journal

not very hip
he never knew that Marx

                  —the German Jew—
had written ". . . those martyrs
are lodged in the great heart
of the working class"

                     useless to try to explain
those were the days of the Commune

        drawn
by cabaret music
the cozy sensation of high society
Gauguin wanted some cash in his pockets
and his feet on the ground
to cast a shadow everyone would respect

Sundays he painted hesitant landscapes

                         —impressionism
no longer a pirouette and the duchesses
of the Third Republic had their Monet—
during the week

he was an upright stockbroker
much praised by M. Arosa
collector of Pissarro and noted connoisseur

in the Bertin office
he is described as a severe young man
impeccable frock coat mustache
a bit provocative but polite
even to his yawn
                    even a little slow
in his responses like the page boys
or the directors of the Bank of France

married in Copenhagen
he had children and went on painting on Sundays

at the Bourse we are told
he grew steadily more remote
and the clients enjoyed commiserating
over this young man once so very promising

no one knows how he managed to break loose
from the early morning embrace of that soft good-natured
body though the bad morning breath
recalls the simple biology
that backs love up
                    nor how he managed
to forget his beginnings
                    —his sons
knew him for a strict father

but human—in short a father
out of a *fin de siècle* manual Advice to Fathers

traveling in Panama
Paris Brussels or Brittany
his brushes fought off
the prickles of any remorse
his right to madness
was confirmed by Vincent Van Gogh
although in Arles everything indicates that they slept
in separate rooms
                  in the Café Voltaire
he tried to understand the poems Mallarmé read aloud
Stéphane was dogged
                  c'était le jour beni
de ton premier baiser
                but Gauguin
remained silent
              he would have liked
to paint those verses but they had no
color not even any human feeling

it wasn't enough
the flight from the Bourse from the
decorous breakfast
the same words repeated endlessly
while the flesh doesn't change

in Tahiti
the authorities look with mistrust

on the white foreigner lover of native girls
they didn't understand that he was trying to objectify
the subjective
             and that the tender
animal warmth of those girls was almost the end
of the road for Paul Gauguin

banished to the Marquesas
he was jailed on suspicion
of not inspiring suspicion
             in Paris
he was put down as a hardened snob
only a few natives knew about his spells
of impotence
             and that "the gold of their bodies"
             was a pretext
for not being forced to think
about the rows of black seats in the Stock Exchange
the cuckoo clock in that dining room in Copenhagen
the voyage to Lima the weeping of his mother
the mannered small talk of the Café Voltaire
             and above all
the incomprehensible poems of Stéphane Mallarmé.

after Vázquez Montalbán

from LINES FOR THE DEATH
OF MY AUNT DANIELA

Daniela's
veins stood out
in the dense
bramble
her frayed stockings
looking for me
pitchblack
those evenings
sitting
on the swing
while I read Lefevbre
Lenin
even
the Holy Family
of Marx
            and Engels
I was thrilled
by their harsh promise
industrial workers
of the world
the red sash would be
a bodice
                 lusty wench
lusty dugs of freedom

like a broken glass
in the silence

she was speaking
she thought she was speaking
she was only remembering

the shoemaker
had dreamed of being a bullfighter

what a small face
what bewildered eyes
what a knowing shudder
the trembling of her lips
before my silence

afterwards
the spinal column
crumbling away
in the hospital
there were traces of Gaudí's genius
or his disciples
the great windows
looked out over a garden
almost
almost British
an acacia
was combing its hair
above her bedstead

the shoemaker said
she could not last the winter
in nineteen hundred

fifty-
nine
Elvis Presley
landed in Spain

              new St. James

for the first time
refrigerators
congealed
puddings
and crabs
the Sacred Heart
became a penholder
and Di Stéfano
confirmed with one kick
the hegemony
of Real Madrid

I was praying
for the earthly paradise
that night
while
the acacia's hair was coming down
in confusion
and Gaudí's genius
was overwhelmed
by the visionary
vertigo of death
the sea
of 1910
an imperial hussar

black tempests
drowned the air
black clouds
kept them from seeing
        past the barricades
past the parapets
the leaves of the rationbooks
were flying
the waxen face
        of a shoemaker

fresh
the ink on the balls
of my fingers
fresh marks
in the book
where everything is written
I heard the Latin
in sullen misery

her body laid out
obscenely
reactionary
on the slab
on one leg
the darning
resembled the scars
of some recent wound

the city grew
from the cemetery

with a rhythm you could see
possibly

           miraculous

a young Werther
of tempered steel
I prayed to the most
dialectical gods:

              proletarians

of the world
star seekers
I await you some day
under a sky that clouds over
that place where
your fallen sister dwells
in alien earth

you will carry the flag
of the darned sock
and just beyond your fist
fear of the earth

no
don't let the dead
come back

           never again

will anyone believe
in their oceanic
hands
in their golden reign
avenging vines

that strangle monstrous
sons
in cold blood

stupidly
material   death
calls into question
antibiotics
climates
medicinal waters
the reputations
of specialists specializing
in extremely special
specialties

calls into question
progress ascending
                    altogether
too much skin
contact
body heat or glances
prolonging
their aftermath
the wisdom
of hours written off
run run
stiff patter of
rain
cleaner of windowpanes
life

a puddle or trickle
grey
with city grit
sewers after all
which is death

feeble metaphor
life is no river
nor is it a sewer
it's a dialectic
stream
of wills
over the corpses
of frustrations
              forgotten things
murders
coldblooded and merciful
words
silences
guilts and data
from National Institutes
of Input Output
and Opinion
for those of us who wanted
to build the coming
centuries
neither her brief life
nor her unhappiness
teaches anything
merely her absurdity

the small reach
of her mouth
and her limitations
twist ethics too tight
and set off
ideological crises
overcome
by reading all night
manuals
some poems by Alberti
and above all
the conjuring thought
of Mao Tse Tung

sometimes it grows dark

the world has grown

I leave asleep
everything I have
mine or others'
I remember
how little I loved
that woman who loved me
            and then
I would like to be off
to where
time out of mind
open ports
          await us

and no ships

        to bring us back

life died
memory leaves nothing
to console us

        at present
the means
dirty whatever they touch

        and in the childhood
of man   desire
stimulates growth

        records
the athletes still call them

tomorrow
no doubt
there will not be
such sad stories   just right
for the feelings of the past

       naturally
the washerwomen will be organized
tuberculosis wiped out
and the discrepancies
between abstract and concrete
synthesized
the strength of one man
will be the strength
of all men

       pointless

the good intentions
the nostalgia
the regrets

the memories

after Vázquez Montalbán

Barcelona, 1965–1973

COUPLETS

For plucking the feathers from archangels of the heights,
the delicate snowfall with its slender teeth
is sentenced to the weeping of the fountains
and the desolation of the running springs.

For intermingling its spirit with the metals,
for giving away to iron its sunrises,
powerful blacksmiths drag the fire off
to face the consequences on the ruthless anvils.

Towards the cruel attentions of the thorn
as towards the fatal weakness of the rose,
towards the corrosive action of death itself

I see myself hurled headlong, and all this ruin
is not for any crime, or anything
but loving you, only for loving you.

after Hernández

The fruit is gorged with sweetness past all reason
And the flies come in their hundreds.

Doors opening and closing all night long
But never the right one.

And I used to envy Solomon all those women—
If he was wise, he left them to their own devices.

Nectar rises to the nostril frothy and tingling
And thus the bee is trapped.

I know her better than she knows herself—
Love has conferred on me this trivial privilege.

All night I have lain awake pleading with my heart please
Don't do this to me again.

You never stopped to think why it smelled so good
And you never will.

The eyes close gratefully as the moment ripens,
The tongue searches out its desire in the darkness.

And the arms reach to embrace their own rib cage
And a red absence flashes on the walls of the heart.

You've read a thousand books and what do you know?
Was there some membrane between your eye and the page?

You rummage through the alphabet and the blood
For one word through which the world can be seen.

The odor of women, eyelashes, breasts
Drift now in the starry smoke of memory.

Your eyes were open, but then, so are a blind man's.
So are a dead man's.

Mother is almost gone, father, the children hurry off,
Leaves fly, dust, the season changes.

On the path to the village thousands of wildflowers;
In the sunlight, a young girl drawing water from a well.

Why do we never tire of this story
As if we were hearing it again for the first time?

Mouths searching each other for minutes, years,
Warmer and warmer, looking for the hidden word.

Arms and legs intertwined, skin sliding on skin,
The blood rushing joyously into its channels.

The breasts open their eyes in the darkness of palms,
The eyes widen at every little touch.

The fingers brush against the mouth of the womb
In the conversation of the deaf and blind.

Yoked by flesh, shaking, hollering praises,
Both rise as one body to the opening.

The shining phallus erupts in a spray of stars
Flying into her night at tremendous speed.

If their eyes became the darkness, they would see,
Flaming in the darkness, their blowtorch auras.

Sperm on her lips, her hair, her eyes closed,
His whole body bathed in the odor of the garden,

Wet, motionless, barely breathing,
They fill slowly with the surrounding darkness.

The memory of joy is emptier than these empty bottles,
The hope of it just as vain.

The fragrance of her cunt is the fragrance of eternal love
That doesn't last a second.

These splendors of eye and tongue are what wine means,
And fire, and the journey home.

Yet the coolness of her smile is a hierarchy of locked doors
Behind which women disport themselves.

A lightburst of bubbles from dark tons of water . . .
A dress waving in wind . . .

After the snow melts, the snow man stands a long time,
Then the snow man melts.

And they that have power to hurt do it.
They do not do the thing they most do show.

You have a fancy name for your state of mind—
It's just a kettle banging in the wind.

The heart wants instruction in the realities
And pain is expert.

If you're lost in the woods, you move in circles.
If you're done with the fire you started, put it out.

The poet sits praising himself over and over,
As if it mattered, as if it could be proved.

The lover regards his pleasures as his by right;
He seizes on them, he thinks *they* were what he was after.

If you really have it, you don't have to think about it,
You're not always looking to make it something special.

Otherwise, the bud blackens, the petals fray into themselves.
You do not go into the feast unless you know this.

To conjure what is not there and not see what is
Was only one of your stupendous gifts.

And to vie with another—as if victory
Shone more brightly than our shameless failures.

As everyone says, you're very intelligent.
There must be something wrong with your eyes.

An infant screams in the darkness of the crib;
A man might as well step off the end of the precipice.

If I were you, as I am in more ways than one,
I'd look into my heart, and keep looking.

Tu Fu says a poet's ideas should be simple and noble.
Better yet if the poet is simple and noble.

She thinks if she puts out, her sainthood will be recognized.
He figures his wit and pathos entitle him to love.

She laughs and cries, showing her small teeth;
He lifts her dress and buries his face in her bush.

She loves somebody else, who doesn't give a shit.
He does too, but that's different.

It was all good clean fun that had no future
And now it doesn't even have a past.

Neither of them is even alive at this point—
There's just me, and you, I suppose, wherever you are.

What a mess, the meat burnt, the sink overflowing,
The kid won't stop crying, he wants his milk.

The bee's so bloated with nectar he can't fly,
Buzzing on his back at the flower's foot.

So many fresh blooms! Summer will never end,
The fucking idiot dances in his euphoria.

The first faint brown nibbles at the edge of a leaf—
Even the city cousin notices such things.

Down an aisle of leafy shade and leafy sunlight,
Growing smaller and smaller, she disappears.

The watcher, shivering, cannot believe his eyes
That this body too should be taken away from him.

The dry husk of a stonefly clinging to a rock
Came apart in my fingers, the wind lifted it away.

Ojos que no ven, corazon que no siente—
The little peasant whispers it over and over.

From a thousand Chinese dinners, one cookie:
Good fortune in love, also a better position.

So much for both. Too many humorless people
Who can't believe that God could have made the cunt.

Maybe he didn't make it. Maybe hydrogen
Made nitrogen and one thing led to another.

Some hold that early man stumbled upon it
While dreaming of the perfect end to a long day's hunt.

But I say only Italians, with their flair for drama,
Could have invented this fragrant envelope.

Let's drink to the Italians, especially Catullus,
Who knew it was no joke but couldn't help laughing.

A tear falls wordlessly into darkness.
Slivers of gold light faint on the threads of her bodice.

And terrible longings that can't name themselves
Burrow down through the soul and end up digging into wood.

Seven numbers want to be sucked off;
A guy named Susan is dying alone in her bed.

And look, foam is drying into webs in the beer glass,
It wants to rejoin the air and be free of all this.

You can't die from it but you wish you could.
And even at this moment, you smell your fingers.

From the bus window, banks of filthy snow,
Vivid winter faces, none of them hers.

There's the one who kisses and the one who offers the cheek—
If I'm love's fool, what is she?

Her first resort was to dwell on how young she is—
The younger the more innocent, the bitch.

Why blame her for the glitterings and the scents?
That sensual phosphorescence belongs to no one.

Straining and sweating toward futures that never opened,
You were the favorite slave of your imagination.

Sometimes, in the small hours of the brain,
I feel if I let go of these lines I'd fall to my death.

She's not the only grief, or the heaviest.
I've got ten more right here under my fingernails.

Yet when I turn them over, they're not griefs at all
But far-off lights, a town where we might be happy.

We come from the same town. We used to live there
And must have known once what it meant, without asking.

Remember the depths of her eyes and swimming there.
Remember the glistening festivals of her body.

Remember the sudden chestnut mare and the colt
Running out through buckthorn to the high mountain lake

By which we slept. Remember the fullness of the moon
And the mountains drinking in that sea of milk.

Remember the long silences. Remember the flute
Answering to itself high up on the red cliffs.

Remember the rock floored with sun and two immortals
And the white water crashing and frothing in the channel.

And her arms raised to her hair, lifting the small breasts,
The flat belly, legs akimbo, tuft of fur,

The faint shadow of the wings of the dragonfly—
Remember everything. And now forget it.

The hound keeps circling a putrid lump of fur
But after a while, it gets bored and wanders off.

When the flowers are empty, the bee flies straight home
With no more regret than the setting sun.

Stop crying, lover, you were both well served.
When the bill comes in, someone must pay.

A woman gazes after a man, a man after a woman
But their eyes don't meet. They're looking somewhere else.

Stopping on a deserted street, the shock of seeing
Your half-moon face in the black window.

I see the adjective and the noun entwined,
The verb reaching out its hands to them all.

A line of verse advances into whiteness
With long feelers, like a blind man's cane.

It sings about snow, how warm it is in the snow,
But the next line has something entirely different in mind.

It has the man and the woman, or two men,
And it can scarcely bear to say what it sees.

What did you see in those eyes that made you feel shame
And you wouldn't look but turned your face away?

Black branches whipping, rain streaming down the glass,
A lamp burning beside the empty bed.

The sun had almost buried itself in the grass
Before your shadow leapt off into violet space.

And then the earth disappeared, and there was a stain
Blackening and fading in the emptiness.

Millions of stars look down the speechless dark.
Until finally you too lower your eyes.

In the deep street of the dream, I look up,
Trying to make out a woman's face in a black window.

You can't see anything, and all you can hear
Is a black wind going crazy in the branches.

Just wavering points of light in the hills
And off to one side, maybe half a dozen windows.

The face of Jesus, one side of a flowered bedspread,
False teeth drowning in a glass of water.

What would you say, forty or fifty yards?
The wind on my forehead comes from Andromeda.

Another light goes out in the twig-lashed dark;
Not many people sit up all night around here.

She comes slowly out of the bathroom, takes off her robe,
Sits down in front of the mirror, her face crumbles,

Behind her a man about fifty, with dead eyes—

Suddenly I step through the window

Don't be afraid of dying. The glass of water
Is quickly poured into the waiting goblet.

Your face that will be of no further use to mirrors
Grows more and more transparent, nothing is hidden.

It's night in the remotest provinces of the brain.
Seeing falls back into the great sea of light.

How strange to see that glittering green fly
Walk onto the eyeball, rubbing its hands and praying.

Don't be afraid, you're going to where you were
Before birth pushed you into this cold light.

Lie down here, next to Empedocles;
Be joined to the small grains of the brotherhood.

One, that smiles at echoes and knows it is one.
Two, thrilled, terrified, lost in the fog.

The cold sea that stretches between these lovers
Is wider than the gulf between knowing and not knowing.

What's ignorance but another name for time?
"A time when the thought of the eye made me feel cold . . ."

Our foam and frenzy beats its head against the sea wall,
Although, for a moment there, it seemed . . .

It seems it was a drug, or a recollection,
But no images, only an odor, achingly familiar.

The current passing between the tips of the horns
Burns in the pupils, ripples beneath the black hide.

Yet full of bewildered longing we press to the glass
Toward that far-off light burning in the middle of nowhere.

As soon as the water strikes the dish,
The bauble falls from our hands.

And the car ploughs the invisible like an arrow,
Rain leaps on the highway in slashed, blinding sheets.

How many times have I driven a thousand miles
Only to find the door locked, the shades drawn?

To be in love—stroking toward the bed of the ocean
Where the deeper you swim, the harder it is to see . . .

The house is a shambles, the eyes a little nauseous,
Yet the sunlight still falls amorously on the rug.

Doing the dishes, I turned into my two hands
And they sang to each other, a little sailor's tune . . .

The needle veers back and forth in the last groove.
The faint sound of that fire consumes the whole night.

Spectral rings on the table, the mother's rings,
Whose young body once flashed in the firelight.

Not a breath stirs the mound of cold ashes
That still feathers the curve of the Beloved's face.

Nothing beholds itself in the gilded mirror.
The silence is imaginary with no one there to hear it.

To be that no one, disappeared forever,
Already dancing in the golden chambers of the hive!

A bud opens in the light of the word *green*;
From thick foliage, the first tentative trills.

The mantis aligns itself with what is before it,
Motionless in the leaf-and-stem meditation.

And what if some poet carved his name in these woods
As in the crumbling stone of a prison cell?

The letters sprout garlands of leaves, crowns of wings,
Overgrowth covers up the last scorched face.

Even that girl we spoke of, in headlong flight
Feels her arms burst into blossom and curl upward.

Even the lips, moving silently . . .

In a field of mustard and grasses, blowing light,
A house, almost beyond the light. Who lives in it?

Mother is resting. On Sunday it is so.
The cat's eyes half close. The mice go by unmolested.

Alighting to sip dew from the cool ruffles
The butterfly bows slightly, folding her wings.

There in a stripe of sunlight yellow as her blood,
Spilled wine, and a thimble lying on its side.

Glimpses given even to those in torment.
Yes. Even in this world.

SOME OCCASIONAL POEMS

A JOYFUL NOISE

for the marriage of Matthew Paul and Naomi Mezey

And now the day is come at last, praise be—
Praise be to the Almighty, blessèd be He,
As Abraham praised Him with the ram He sent
And David with a ten-stringed instrument—
Naomi and Matthew have come to reunite,
And may it be acceptable in His sight.
Praise be that ends they were not conscious of
Leafed and bore blossom and a ripening love
(By Chance or Fate, which may be the same thing
As the Almighty) brought them to this spring
To inscribe their names together in the Book.
But Lord, how slow they seemed, how long it took,
This destined marriage, its date forecast, then changed
(One that their parents gladly had arranged,
Had power and custom given them the chance),
But as it happened, this ten-year romance
Grew at its own sweet will, now here, now there,
Thriving past difficulty, doubt and care
(Nothing their anxious parents could do but pray)
At last to bring us to this wedding day.
At any rate, she chose him and he chose her—
Hard to say which of them is luckier.
Joy to them both, and to their friends and kin
(So many hardly another could squeeze in),
Who wish them every good life has in store,
Their paths through flowers fifty years and more,
Nourishing work and love, conjugal peace

(And holy strife sometimes) and, of course, increase.
Let sorrows keep their distance, and the years
Yield up their riches and hold back their tears,
And let us hold back ours, or at least try,
And, giving constant praise to the Most High,
Celebrate these fresh rites and awhile share
The love and happiness of this happy pair—
On whom a father's blessings, which employ,
Once more, *his* ten-stringed instrument of joy.

LAST WORDS

for John Lawrence Simpson, 1897–1969

Like men who meet
for the first time from opposite ends of the earth,
we never talked much.
You sat at the kitchen table, in a chair
only the smallest children dared to sit in,
yelling at your sons or telling some sly story,
or silent, looking out the window
at your cattle lumbering toward the barn
and bushes and saplings bent in the steady wind,
and I sat next to you, hands folded,
staring at your daughter, barely listening,
a writer of books, a poet.

Now what was faithful
most of a century to the earth
and the darkness of earth
is preparing to become the earth,
and what was faithful to the light
is turning painfully into light.
Now I want to say
what I have never said.

Old man, sometimes I felt like a child
sitting next to you.
I watched your hands
that were ropy and twisted as if pulled from the earth

and the blue smoke curling upward in the silence
and felt like a child.

There were many things I didn't understand.
How easily fooled I was
by your fierceness, your long silences,
your rants against communism,
your scorn for tender minds.
How easily I assumed
your distaste for my long hair and long face
and long history of childhood.
Still, I listened to your stories

and I remember well
the mules straining in the darkness, the bitter thin air,
the mountain road deep in snow, the huge logs
half hidden in snow, and snow coming down,
and summer nights in the old days,
wild girls riding bareback over the foothills,
sisters of local rustlers going to a dance,
and your old Harley hitting a big hole
and going down sliding sideways in the gravel,

and I remember what I saw,
long after midnight in the cold shed,
the long rip in the cow's side,
the silent man in shirtsleeves, arm
plunged in up to the shoulder, the cow's head
secured in the iron stanchions, her eyes
black and rolling in terror,

the cloud of her breath, the cloud of mine,
not a sound, blood everywhere,
I remember what I saw in your eyes.

And I see drifting through the valley fog
the cool sun—
through the wreckage of years, cars,
dead pigeons, dead wives,
good deals and foolish charity,
money made and lost,
made again and lost again,
a dead baby, a dead son growing rich in the East,
the leaves withering on the vine,
the dying sun,
through death and divorce and dull disaster,
a young and tender spirit.

The road is paved,
the hole filled in,
the girls lie under the stones of Academy Cemetery
many years.
All the old mountain men
gone for good into the mountains,
the sound of their laughter growing very faint,
and the wind keeps blowing.

JOE SIMPSON

Joe Simpson was a man I scarcely knew.
I saw him when he came to see his father.
Our talks, if they were talks, were brief and few.
And yet I think I knew the man, or rather,
I knew something about him. From his eyes
A certain light (though uncertain to me)
Seemed to precede him through the world of lies,
Flickering shadows where he could not see
What might await, what ecstasies of pain,
What narrow passages, where only faith,
That cannot know what it is faithful to,
Can find the right path to the gates of death,
A path he followed, and did not complain,
A path that might lead nowhere, as he knew.

APRIL FOURTH

I throw open the door
And someone like the night walks in

A moist wind in the doorway
A breath of flowers
In the wake of this august presence

I was sitting for hours
Watching the coal
Of the cigarette rising and falling
Finally one must do something

The evening I thought
The evening was the last evening
As usual

I was thinking of heroes
Whose knuckles shine as they curl round a rifle
I was thinking of my brother
Who brings me my head in a basket
What is there to do

Let me make myself empty
I can live without sleeping tonight

I can live without dreams of the King
Awash on his balcony
Half of his face and neck in another kingdom

In the morning I will not understand

Mountains surfacing from the mortal darkness
A scum of yellow flowers
The great oak crying with a thousand voices

All that
Wrinkles like heat and disappears into thin air

BREATHING YOU

in memory of Robert Ockene

I take up your hookah
lovingly fashioned from this and that,
wee perfume bottle, copper fittings,
a thin surgical tube, a bit of ivory,
and clean the wire mesh bowl clogged with old ash,
and cut a few crumbs from the hard black molar of hash,
and hold a flame to it till it glows alive,
and breathe in
your sweetness, sweeter than hash, breath
held till I think
perhaps I am dead
and can look for you now in the rising smoke
in the first rains of winter
your young widow's face
in my hands the hive
the bee's flight of your love
in smoke disappearing like water in water
or good in good
and find you
                    and lose you again
in my lungs in my blood

breathing you.

ON THE RETIREMENT OF THE SCHOLAR, THOMAS PINNEY

Is an earl lower than a duke?
Was Graham Greene a British spook?
A wig the same as a peruke?
 Don't ask me—ask Pinney.

What's an advowson? What's a scrum?
Where did the Mercians come from?
Why did Auden call Tennyson dumb?
 You'd better go ask Pinney.

What's a *bandar*? What's a *drong*?
Did T. E. Lawrence use a bong?
And the Long Parliament—how long?
 I don't know—ask Pinney.

Did Surrey write the first blank verse?
Who or what was Scotland's Curse?
To whom was Anthony Adverse?
What was the name of Juliet's nurse?
Did Coleridge ever *once* converse?
What the hell is a marriage-hearse?
 Jesus Christ!—ask Pinney.

Was wine made earlier than beer?
Did shamans ever interfere?
When did winos first appear?
 Please!—ask Professor Pinney.

Did Oliver Goldsmith really gibber?
Was Aphra Behn a Women's Libber?
What kind of dog is Colly Cibber?
    Don't ask me—ask Pinney.

Why did Wordsworth go to seed?
Who reasoned, "Reason not the need"?
How Venerable *was* the Bede?
Does anyone read Herbert Read?
Why did John go to Runnymede?
Was Walter Raleigh high on weed?
    Enough, enough!—ask Pinney.

Did Wilde and Whistler like each other?
Was Jesse Henry James's brother?
When did the Heights begin to wuther?
    I don't know—ask Pinney.

What was the value of a guinea?
Why was Shelley such a ninny?
What did Crane mean by *findrinny*?
    God only knows—and Pinney.

A RETIREMENT POEM
FOR DICK BARNES

Translating, editing, doing research;
Doing his job and doing kindnesses,
Acts of devotion, though outside of church;
Cherishing everything, which is all there is;
Year after year to almost no one's knowledge,
Devising verses to give strangers pleasure,
In the obscurity of Pomona College
Himself not knowing he's a national treasure;
One of the roughs, but noble in courtesy,
Suffering gladly fool and anæsthete;
A friend to young, fresh folk, and friend to me,—
Let him withdraw now to his high retreat,
Some leafy and sun-dappled bower, from where
He may gaze out upon the passing fair.

EDGAR

I said to you once, "Wasn't Henri lucky?
I'd like to go the easy way he went,
Suddenly, in the middle of the night."
And you replied, "Oh no, I want to *be* there."

And so you were. There, infinitely far.

A PRAYER FOR THE EIGHTH DAY

O Lord of life, it is our joy
To bring before You this small boy.
He bears the name of a great son,
A clever and a favored one;
Give him another name as well,
That of his namesake—Israel,
And gather him into Your fold,
Your chastened people as of old.
Let him deal justly; let him be
Forgiving, self-forgetful, free;
But let him never forget You
And worship clay as the heathen do.
Make him a good man, and a Jew.

INTERLUDE:
MORE CLERIHEWS

Said Charles Baudelaire
To Jeanne Duval, "Ma chére,
There have been rumors
That you don't wear bloomers."

Against Gertrude Stein
We have to hold the line.
Her influence on contemporary verse
Could hardly be worse.

William Cullen Bryant
Was certainly not a giant,
But deserves a passing mention
For *To the Fringèd Gentian.*

Yvor Winters
Reduced his cudgels to splinters,
But all in a good cause,
Enforcing the metrical laws.

Marianne Moore
Was prim and rather dour,
Not at all the sort of poetess
You might interest in coitus.

Paul Verlaine
Liked a boy now and again,
But Li'l Arthur gave him rather more
Than he bargained for.

Paul Gauguin
Was a ladies' man.
He loved them in Tahiti and Provence.
Honi soit qui mal y pense.

Friedrich Nietzsche
Was a very strange crietzsche:
He dreamt of mounting a little wench
And screaming "Übermensch!"

Jonathan Swift
Was continually miffed,
But what really drove him out of his mind
Was the thought of Stella wiping her behind.

Charles Bukowski
Could never find his housekey,
But being a total souse,
He was lucky just to find his house.

Lawrence of Arabia
Had little interest in labia.
No, his idea of joy
Was a slender brown Bedouin boy.

Homer
Is no misnomer—
The first superstar,
Nobody has ever hit one as far.

Walter Savage Landor
Was a powerful left-hander.
With more than one perfect game,
He should be in the Hall of Fame.

William Butler Yeats
Was one of the near-greats;
If he hasn't dined with Landor and that bunch,
He has at least had lunch.

Robert Herrick
Was a foxy old cleric—
Concerned for the state of his soul,
Yet dearly loving his jellyroll.

Dylan Thomas
Never fulfilled his early promise;
He wrote some amusing prose,
But that's as far as it goes.

D. H. Lawrence
Put on some weight in Florence,
But got skinnier
When he went to Sardinia.

James Fenimore Cooper
Was a real trooper:
He ground dozens of novels out
Without even knowing what he was talking about.

The Earl of Surrey
Was too highborn to worry,
But moving from bed to bed,
He was bound to lose his head.

George Herbert, John Donne—
You could pick either one.
And what about Sir Philip Sydney?
He wrote some good poems, didney?

William Morris
Was no Horace,
But (sigh)
Neither am I.

EVENING WIND
AND OTHER POEMS

EVENING WIND

One foot on the floor, one knee in bed,
Bent forward on both hands as if to leap
Into a heaven of silken cloud, or keep
An old appointment—tryst, one almost said—
Some promise, some entanglement that led
In broad daylight to privacy and sleep,
To dreams of love, the rapture of the deep,
Oh, everything, that must be left unsaid—

Why then does she suddenly look aside
At a white window full of empty space
And curtains swaying inward? Does she sense
In darkening air the vast indifference
That enters in and will not be denied,
To breathe unseen upon her nakedness?

after an etching by Edward Hopper

NO WAY

I thought I heard someone calling.
Honey. Was I asleep?
Suddenly there you were,
Your yellow hair shaking,
Voicing the anger of life.
You said I must leave this house,
Whosoever it was. Not mine. Not yours.
And I did. I went right out
Into a courtyard. Some sort of courtyard.
Impassive brick rising higher and higher.
No way out. No way back in.

FRAGMENTS OF AN ENDLESS GHAZAL

How did I get so lucky? I don't know—
I'll have to ask my rich and famous friend.

Was it just yesterday I was in seventh heaven,
Somewhere in the vicinity of her sanctum?

Rings on your fingers, soft pigskin on your feet,
You've got the world by the tail, like a dead cat.

Shoes have no illusions. One by one
They wear down to where there are no more footsteps.

Yet still the Queen disappears into the brilliance—
Born to pursue her, you can't refuse.

*   *   *

Only a fool would leave himself defenseless,
But how will your lover come into the heart's fortress?

What does he lose but a skin of innocence
That grows back almost as soon as it gets ripped off?

Did you only imagine she gave herself body and soul?
Came a time she wouldn't give you the time of day.

Ah, love's a treasure and love's a pleasure . . .
Better decide if that makes two loves, or one.

The bee spreads those petals for his food—
If that's the food of love, baby, just play on.

How many times must you be sick, boy,
Before you see that the world is not an oyster?

* * *

How delicious this pain is! never again
To lie in the arms of the daughter of the Prophet.

While I was loving her madly, I said little,
Just let my body sink down into her dark waters.

But she gave me three kinds of wine, red, white, and yellow,
And they poisoned my heart. My darling, I only dreamt this.

Is it possible I arranged for all this to happen,
So I could be happy with my wretched poems?

Listen, friend, I'll tell you what I think:
I think these little murders are very well planned.

SLOW SONNET

Nothing is sometimes better than something.
There are extremes—of boredom, thirst, fear, pain.
At one extreme the sky is darkening.
Through shafts of sun it has begun to rain.
Soon it will be over; that's its nature.

Now it is over and so too is the sun.
Now what, a sleep, a drink, a double feature?
There are things you can't say to anyone.
Few words have ever made it to the heart.
They say the feelings are best dulled by work.
Maybe we can hide out awhile in art.
Be quiet now. It is completely dark.

Consciousness can barely keep its balance.
Now it is falling into a dense silence.

LAÏS DEDICATES TO APHRODITÊ THE TOOLS OF HER TRADE

Words cannot say what she was in her prime,
This Laïs, now a specimen of Time.
She used to laugh to see so many men,
Not one of whom she'll ever see again.

Goddess, to you I yield my useless mirror—
What can it do but verify Time's error?
It will not show me as I used to be,
And what it will show I refuse to see.

after an anonymous poet

CHIN MUSIC

We listen, *Mucus*, as you sing the blues—
You've paid, are paying, and will pay your dues;
You'll sing till the conversion of the Jews.
But misery wears thin at such a rate,
And, sympathetic as we are, it's late.
No more, we whisper, and we say, Take care,
And miles away, add gratefully, There, there.

He likes to introduce his "better half"
(With an ironic chuckle). What a laugh.
Better or worse, it's not much of a boast:
It makes her half of nothing, at the most.

Feminum dreams of leading a jihad:
She'll be the scourge of Nature, Man, and God.
Down with the enemies of *Feminum*!
Woe to the oglers of her lovely bum!
Death to gold-diggers, men who still can come,
And any other heterosexual scum!

Minor is growing old. He wants to save
Some vestige from the black hole of the grave.
He scans the learned journals, the reviews,
The reams of rude or elegant abuse,
He takes in whole biographies at a glance—
What happiness if a page or two perchance

Should mention him in passing, maybe quote,
And for a headstone rear the long footnote.

Prudent, for giving less and getting more,
Winds up on the wrong side of a locked door.
And what's his profit, when push comes to shove?
The wages of three-quarter-hearted love.

Devious loves to give you a bum steer
(Cover your back when he is most up front)—
He tells you what he thinks you want to hear
Or what he thinks you think he thinks you want.

Suckling is young—he wants the world his oyster,
The wine ever drier, and the women moister.
He would have drowned rather than board the Ark,
The stench of animals, the cold, the dark.

Yet once more, O ye patriots, and once more,
The tribal fife and drum of holy war,
The call to heroism and martyrdom—
But count me out. Incognito, ergo sum.

Rulers of all sorts swear they cherish Peace;
They sing her praises, kiss her, stroke her fleece.
Yet if she will not yield to their Desire,
They rape her, cut her throat, set her on fire.

TO THE AMERICANS

Not till every blackened church has been rebuilt,
and you have repented in dust and ashes—
      of God mocked in the universities,
    blasphemous jokes in the chic galleries,

repented, even though you yourself be guiltless,
of covetous hearts, of ears uncircumcised,
      deaf to others' pain, of worshiping
    wealth and filth, of overweening power,—no,

not till you call to mind the ancient mystery:
only obedience to Him commands obedience,
      will you face your shame, Americans,
    and only then begin to make amends.

You have already faced the Lord's fierce anger,
faced the humiliation of being forced
      to watch one of your sons, a naked
    corpse dragged through the dust of Mogadishu,

all around him the faces of his killers,
grinning savages, one wearing his dog tags;
      and bombed-out embassies, innocent
    Africans butchered for your fathers' sins;

and our own streets in flames, drifting with tear gas,
tears for the future. The long oozings of lust,

rage and rebellion steeped three decades,
the venom gathering strength month by month,

—until today, the nubile preteen reveling
in hip-hop, her virginity twenty times lost
(discarded, rather), lies dreaming of
what new taste-thrill? whips? threesomes? Whatever.

Meanwhile, one who could be her older sister,
her mother even, stands ready to open
her scented privacies to a stranger,
some stockbroker buddy of her husband's

(and her husband knows: he was the go-between!)
Cunt on the house. Or else she's off on her own—
what fun to find her own whoremaster,
lift her skirts to him in her marriage bed.

Not from such unclean loins did the lean farmboys,
the hardbitten wranglers and factory stiffs spring
who waded ashore at Normandy,
those the bullets hadn't yet cut in half—

no, those who bled for and saved us, those who died
in the Solomons, in the Ardennes, in the sky,
tough, God-fearing young men who sweated
blood in the blast furnace, rode the tractor

long past sundown, or else rode the rods, cooking
a thin slumgullion in the hobo jungles
      or sold windfall fruit on grey sidewalks,
    thin shirts and sharp faces against winter,

they came of better stock. May God have mercy.
Their grandchildren, so licentious, so greedy,
      go on dancing, drinking and snorting,
    lovelessly fucking, all frantic, manic—

Degeneration doesn't come suddenly
to an end; shrugged at, accepted, it takes over.
      Who will die to save *their* grandchildren,
    come face to face once more with real evil?

                  after Horace

THE NOBLE RIDER AND THE SOUND OF WORDS: A CENTO

*"I might be expected to speak of the social, that is
to say sociological or political obligations of the poet.
He has none."*

The soul no longer exists and we droop in our flight.
If only we could yield ourselves to the unreal—
But we cannot yield, we are not free to yield.
Still on the edge of the world in which we live
Is an invincible man, who moves in our midst,
Traversing vacant space like the empty spirit,
Smoke-drift of puffed-out heroes,
Or is it perhaps a rider intent on the sun,
Rushing from what is real? It is gorgeous nonsense,
Dear, gorgeous nonsense, the passion of rhetoric.
The enemies of poetry like Freud
Despise the consolation of illusion,
Without which men cannot endure reality,
The cruelty of it. They would have us
Venture into the hostile world, which is,
The way we live and the way we work alike,
A world of ever-enlarging incoherence,
Of violence, the disparagement of reason,
Absent of any authority save force,
The spirit of negation being so active.
We lie in bed and listen to a broadcast,
The drift of incidents, to which we accustom ourselves
As to the weather, the impermanence of the future

And of the past—as for the present,
It is merely an opportunity to repent.
Little of what we believed is true—
Only the prophecies are true:
The movement of people in the intervals of a storm,
A whole generation and a world at war,
And the war only a part of a warlike whole
Beyond our power to tranquilize.
But for the possible poet, the noble rider
Responsive to the most minute demand,
The dead are still living,
Living on the earth or under it,
And what is dead lives with an intensity
Beyond any experience of life,—
Black water breaking into reality.
This potent figure cannot be too noble,
The arm of bronze outstretched against all evil.
Don Quixote will make it imperative
For him to choose between the imagination
And brute reality. His choice must be
That they are equal and inseparable.
It is not enough to cover the rock with leaves.
But neither is everything favorable to reality.
The use of that bare word has been enough;
It means something to everyone, so to speak.
Reality is things as they are,
The life that is lived in the scene that it composes,
It is a jungle in itself,
A plainness of plain things, a savagery.
It became violent and so remains,

Wherefore the possible poet must resist
Its pressure, and with the violence within
Protect us from the violence without,
Always in emptiness that would be filled.
One loves and goes back to one's ancient mother
Certainly not as a social obligation
But out of a suasion not to be denied.
Who is it that the poet addresses? Stalin
Might grind his teeth the whole of a Russian winter,
And the poets might be silent in the spring.
Who is it that the poet addresses? A drab?
Or a woman with the hair of a pythoness?
To give life whatever savor it possesses,
By some fortune of the mind give it that life
For which it was searching and which it had not found,
To mate his life with life, to find the real,
To be stripped of every fiction except one—
This is his task. Nothing more difficult
Than the affirmations of nobility:
We turn away from it, as from a grandeur that was,
As something that was noble in its day,
A lifeless rhetoric now false and ugly,
A cemetery of nobilities.
The space is blank space, the objects have no shadows
And exert a mournful power in this poverty.
We live in a place that is not our own,
Not in the world where we shall come to live.
He denies that he *has* a task, but it is he
Who must create the world to which we turn
Incessantly and without knowing it,

With a deepening need for words, for the poem
That is part of the *res* itself and not about it,
All the truth we shall ever experience.
The imagination is nobility.
It cannot be defined, that would fix it,
And to fix it is to put an end to it.
We have been a little insane about the truth.
Poetry is words and words are sounds
Of things that do not exist without the words,
Words that are life's voluble utterance.
We search the sound of words for a finality,
A perfection, an unalterable vibration
In the ecstatic freedom of the mind,
A life that is fluent in even the wintriest bronze.

TO MY FRIENDS IN THE ART

Flyweight champions, may you live
The proverbial thousand years
To whatever smiles and cheers
Flyweight audiences may give.

Ounce for ounce as good as any,
Modest few among the many,
Swift, precise, diminutive,
Flyweight champions, may you live.

ONE-RIME DREAM

I felt the familiar sadness still, my faithful hanger-on,
Remembering with what access of joy how I used to run
In skinny boyhood like the wind, far from everyone.

It may be from the beginning I was beginning to be the one
To do all this solitary, with neither daughter nor son,
Only this book, be what it may, to spare from oblivion.

(And yet its pages are haunted by a mother and a son—
For all their bitter laughter, however they carry on,
They are, it suddenly seems, a way the work of life gets done.)

I was in a freezing courtyard with some nameless infantrymen;
I was kneeling for forgiveness at the hidden feet of a nun;
I was waking in a cold sweat, the sentence unbegun.

AFTER TEN YEARS

Now that the sum of footsteps given you
to walk upon the earth has been fulfilled,
I say that you have died. I too have died.
I, who recall the very night we made
our laughing, unaware farewells, I wonder
what on earth has become of those two young men
who sometime around 1957
would walk for hours, oblivious of the snow
that slashed around those street corners like knives
under the lamps of that midwestern town,
or sit in bars, talking about the women,
or decades later, stroll the perfumed streets
of Pasadena, talking about the meters.
Brother in the felicities of the Herberts,
George and Zbigniew, and of Chivas Regal,
and the warm rooms of the pentameter,
discoverer, as we all were in those days,
of that timeworn utensil, metaphor,
Henri, my tipsy, diffident old friend,
if only you were here to share with me
this empty dusk, however impossibly,
and help me to improve these lines of verse.

after Borges

SPRING EVENING BY WALNUT CREEK

Hey you frogs! You know
A poet name of Bashō?
No? Well, he knows you.

FROM A SKETCHBOOK:
FRAGMENTS AND EPIGRAMS

Adultery, booze, or meth,
They're all of them likely to hurt you;
The wages of sin is death.
But then, so is the wages of virtue.

What is to be my subject for today?
I have no subject; I am nothing's king.
My guilt and torpor keep the world at bay
And are oblivious of everything.

200 gulls facing into the wind
nothing to do but wait for the day's garbage
Ray says, "In all these years
I never seen 'em fuck."

sandpiper playing the waves
out and back on his quick little sticks
lunch on the run
eat up, little sandpiper
the sun that is now so bright on the combers' backs
is falling out of the sky

Invisible hatred or love, I ask your name
And whether you were here all afternoon—
An endless afternoon, and endless rain,
And now this sudden tryst in an empty room.

NEW YEAR'S EVE, 1999

Goodbye, old year. I guess I have seen worse.

crossing under the streetlamp
our shadows meet and part simultaneously
our hearts too

I do not know the secret but it knows me
And drives me to go on talking and wait and see,
Like a child drawing an apocalypse in crayon—
Or a faith healer of little faith, hot to lay on
Hands or call on Jesus, in the hope
He'll know what to do when he reaches the end of his rope.

Words should not be alone too much. They brood,
They start drinking and are never heard from again.

I raise my mind's eye to the invisible,
a dark I could not even begin to describe,
that I know nothing about, will never see,
thinking Lord, Lord, be merciful to this scribe.
But Lord is just a word, and mercy is rare,
and as for the scribe, what in the world is he
who is praying in words here now to nameless nothing
and hasn't got a prayer?

AN UNKNOWN GRAVE

Here by the roadside, subject to no date,
Free of the miseries of love and hate,
And careless, rests a bondservant of fate,
Now the vague dust these lines commemorate.

RUSH HOUR

multitudes machined
for high speed and freedom, all
motionless, fuming

How beautiful civilization is at night,
Seen from a certain height.

HE'LL GROW UP TO BE AN IDIOT JUST LIKE YOU

So my grandfather said, the day my father
Brought me, a raw red infant bundled up
Against the bitter winds of early March,
To show him . . . no, to prove to him that . . . no—
To get the approval hopelessly withheld?
To ask his blessing? I have no idea;
I wasn't really there. In any case,
He was mistaken. I grew up to be
A different sort of idiot entirely.

There is a sound of someone breathing. Sun
Falls like a thought behind a mountain's brow—
The old life over, the new life unbegun,
And nothing more to say. At least for now.

OWL

Nightlong waiting and listening, being schooled
To long lying awake without thoughts,
I hear him calling from the other world.
A long silence, and then two flutey notes—
The cry of nobody, but urgent, cool,
Full of foreboding. He's in the cedar tree
Not twenty feet beyond my windowsill;
The other world is very far away.
When, toward morning, he ceases, the air seems
More visible, although it's not yet light,
The black sky drained and all our speechless dreams
Fading into thought. Lord of the night,
Thy kingdom in which everything is one,
Grant me that sleep that is denied to none.

A SERIOUS NOTE

Staying up late last night,
I opened the screen door
And stepped outside the light
To look for a star or two.
But stars were few to find,
Those I was looking for,
With eyes a little blind
In the too luminous blue
And soft suburban glow;
And the moon's expressionless O
I used to think expressed
Bewilderment and woe
Was merely drifting through
A drifting wrack of cloud
Directly overhead.
An egg in a flimsy nest?
Or a half-covered breast
In its rumpled habitat?
I almost spoke aloud,
Say what you mean tonight,
But light was all it said—
What can I say but light
And reflected light at that?
Let that be my failing.
So, with a sigh, I bent
To earth and undergrowth
Where I stood, inhaling

The breath of leaf and flower
Spread unseen at my feet,
An overpowering scent
That seemed to me, in truth,
My own sweet life in bloom—
As if one could be both,
Sweetness, and all that it meant
To say that it was sweet—
And under the rich perfume
Was something rank and sour.
No, none of this was mine;
There were the shapes of trees,
Cypress and cedar and pine
Motionless in the breeze,
Green to the black power
Against the pale night sky;
And there, as well, was I.
Who heard, I thought, a thrush
Whistling its artless song
In the oleander bush
Or in the cedar tree,
Brilliant, fluent and free
With never a note wrong.
It was a bewitching air.
But thrushes are pretty rare
In this neck of the woods
And most of our neighborhoods—
It must be some other bird.
And suddenly I knew,
Even before it flew,

Just who it was I heard—
Whoever she wanted to call,
Clearly it wasn't me,
For even as she ascended,
The little mockingbird,
On some invisible mission,
One would have had to be blind
Not to see that derision
Was the last thing she had in mind.
In all innocence,
That was how it ended.
And the best joke of all,
A joke at my own expense,
Was to end on a serious note,
One not intended to be
Misunderstood by me,
Out of a mockingbird's throat.

HARDY

Thrown away at birth, he was recovered,
Plucked from the swaddling-shroud, and chafed and slapped,
The crone implacable. At last he shivered,
Drew the first breath, and howled, and lay there, trapped
In a world from which there is but one escape
And that forestalled now almost ninety years.
In such a scene as he himself might shape,
The maker of a thousand songs appears.

From this it follows, all the ironies
Life plays on one whose fate it is to follow
The way of things, the suffering one sees,
The many cups of bitterness he must swallow
Before he is permitted to be gone
Where he was headed in that early dawn.

TEA DANCE AT THE NAUTILUS HOTEL
(1925)

The gleam of eyes under the striped umbrellas—
We see them still, after so many years,
(Or think we do)—the young men and their dears,
Bandying forward glances as through masks
In the curled bluish haze of panatellas,
And taking nips from little silver flasks.

They sit at tables as the sun is going,
Bent over cigarettes and lukewarm tea,
Talking small talk, gossip and gallantry,
Some of them single, some husbands and wives,
Laughing and telling stories, all unknowing
They sit here in the heyday of their lives.

And some then dance off in the late sunlight,
Lips brushing cheeks, hands growing warm in hands,
Feet gliding at the lightest of commands,
All summer on their caught or sighing breath
As they whirl on toward the oncoming night,
And nothing further from their thoughts than death.

But they danced here sixty-five years ago!—
Almost all of them must be underground.
Who could be left to smile at the sound
Of the oldfangled dance tunes and each pair
Of youthful lovers swaying to and fro?
Only a dreamer, who was never there.

after a watercolor by Donald Justice

VARIATION ON A THEME

My hands have made this monument—
Bronze will tarnish before it will.
Smaller than all the glass towers,
Winds cannot shake it, even the strongest,
And the rains powerless, rain and time,
The endless dripping of the years
That wears down everything to nothing.
This body will go down to dust,
But death not touch these slender lines.
As long as boys make war and girls
Bow to the biddings of the goddess,
As long as my native city stands
And one forgotten neighborhood
And the sluggish Delaware flows on,
I shall not altogether perish,
Who helped to keep the meters live.
The honor, if any, will not be mine;
Not mine but yours, creator spirit,
Yours the shaping hands, the laurel.

after Horace

NOTES

A Bedtime Story—Stanley Ketchel was one of the great middleweight champions; of his 52 professional victories, 49 were by knockout. Eating breakfast one morning in 1910, he was shot in the back by an intolerant cuckold. He was twenty-four. The old man in the next stanza is of course Tithonus.

Dream of an Invitation is based on Catullus' *Carmina*, XXXII, *Dream of Departure* on XLVI, and *On a Theme of Sappho's* on LI (which is itself a translation of a lyric by Sappho).

Corinna in Vendôme—This playful title is my invention, moving the Corinna of Herrick's *carpe diem* poem into Ronsard's town in northern France.

The Ballad of Charles Starkweather—This was at least partly a communal effort, composed in Iowa City a few days after Starkweather's execution. That murder spree was the grisliest of the late fifties. Except for the disputed degree of his girlfriend's complicity and the manner of his capture, the facts, based as they were on contemporary newspaper reports, have turned out to be surprisingly accurate, if only by the generous standards of the heroic ballad. Donald Justice contributed a number of lines and phrases—a stanza or two if memory serves—and very likely a word here and there was thrown in by Kim Merker and Henri Coulette and other boisterous beer-drinking friends.

No Country You Remember—I took the title from the last line of an early poem by Peter Everwine.

The Mercy of Sorrow—Uri Zvi Greenberg was born in Lvov in 1896, emigrated to Palestine in 1924, and died in Israel in 1991.

One Summer—In those days, the 1940s, the *Bulletin* was Philadelphia's evening paper.

Prose and Cons—The epigraph is the last words, which may be apocryphal, of John Dillinger as he lay mortally wounded in front of the Biograph Theater in Chicago in 1934. Most of the wordplay in the little prose amusements is clear enough, but there are three extended puns: one plays on Milton's, "They also serve who only stand and wait," and two on the Latin tags, "Mens sana in corpore sano" and "lacrimae rerum."

The Door Standing Open—The epigraph comes from *The Power within Us* (also published as *Interlinear to Cabeza de Vaca*) by Haniel Long.

Terezín was a garrison town forty miles north of Prague, turned into a concentration camp, a junction en route to the death camps. Many thousands of Jewish children were held there, marked eventually for the trains to Auschwitz; only a few hundred survived the war. "SILVIN VI 25 VI 1944," the signature at the bottom of the doomed girl's watercolor, probably includes her barrack number.

Small Song—The epigraph is from Christopher Smart's *Jubilate Agno*.

Last Days in Salt Lake City —"The last malcontent poet" is the Wobbly songwriter and organizer Joe Hill, framed on a homicide charge in Salt Lake City and executed there by firing squad.

Unsent Letter to Luis Salinas—Omar (the Crazy Gypsy), as he is usually known to himself and his friends, is a wildly imaginative and unfortunately little known poet who lives in Fresno.

N. W. is based on a sonnet by Jorge Luis Borges called *J. M.*

Clerihews and Other Sports—Some of these clerihews were begun or finished among friends. Donald Justice contributed several phrases, and Miller Williams generously gave me the amusing rhyme for Sydney.

Tailgaters is another gift from Miller Williams—the name he coined for these comic verses. The only other name I know (also a good one) was reported to me by John Hollander, who says that William Cole used *Uncoupled Couplets* for a collection of such verses.

Her Sparrow is based on Catullus' *Carmina,* III, *Jerry's Stretch* on LXXXVIII, and *All in the Family* on LXXXIX.

Glosses and Variations—The dates of the Greek and Roman poets, Catullus and the makers of *Ancient Epigrams,* range from the fifth century BCE to the sixth century CE. Otherwise, this sequence, which might also be called "impersonations," is in chronological order. Moses ibn Ezra, Abraham ibn Ezra, and Judah Halevi were eleventh- and twelfth-century poets in Moorish Spain. Sor Juana Inés de la Cruz was a self-educated nun in late seventeenth-century Mexico. All of the subsequent glosses and variations are on nineteenth- and twentieth-century poems.

Two Versions of the Emperor's Epigram—The Emperor is Hadrian; he is said to have composed his epitaph a little while before his death. Some scholars have doubted the ascription, but Howard Jackson has made a persuasive argument for its authenticity.

Julio Campal—The Spanish alphabet has twenty-eight letters.

Gauguin—The painter, whose mother was partly Peruvian, visited Peru as a child. After France's disastrous defeat by Prussia in 1871, Adolphe Thiers negotiated a peace with Bismarck and later in the same year ordered his troops to attack the Commune of Paris, an order they carried out with extreme ferocity. Thiers would shortly become president of the Third Republic.

Lines for the Death of My Aunt Daniela—This long excerpt is the last 254 lines of a poem almost four times as long, which I first read in tattered typescript in the late sixties; government permission to publish was refused until after Franco's death. Despite its often obscure allusions and other difficulties, it was widely known and admired in its *samizdat* existence for having given an eloquent voice to the bitter grief and suffering of the Spanish people in the terrible years after the Civil War. Exploiting the resources of classic Spanish elegy (its very title echoing Manrique's *Coplas por la Muerte de Su Padre*), as well as modernist devices, mixing literary diction with the language of the streets, of film and popular song, advertising and propaganda, and moving back and forth from personal elegy to historical judgment, prophetic lamentation and anathema, the poem mourns not only Tia Daniela but also the nation and the destruction of a whole culture. "The shoemaker" is Daniela's husband; "St. James" (St. James the Greater) is Santiago, the patron saint of Spain; and "Di Stéfano" was the star of the Royal Madrid soccer team in the early fifties.

Couplets—The epigraph is based on a poem by Miguel Hernández. The Spanish proverb, "Ojos que no ven, corazon que no siente" ("Eyes that don't see, heart that doesn't feel") is equivalent to our saying, "What you don't know won't hurt you." The reference to Empedocles seemed especially apt because of his images of the continuous dispersal and mingling of all elements. "A time when the thought of the eye made me feel cold" comes from Charles Darwin's notebooks. Several lines in the sequence quote or echo Shakespeare and La Rochefoucald, among others. My large debt to Ghalib and Catullus should be obvious.

April Fourth is, of course, April 4, 1968.

On the Retirement of the Scholar, Thomas Pinney—If the reader is curious to know the answers to any of the questions, he will have to ask Mr. Pinney.

A Retirement Poem for Dick Barnes—The late Dick Barnes was one of our finest poets and translators.

A Prayer for the Eighth Day—A Jewish boy is inducted into the tribe of Israel on the eighth day after his birth.

Fragments of an Endless Ghazal consists of rewritten outtakes from *Couplets.*

Laïs Dedicates to Aphroditê the Tools of Her Trade has been often but wrongly ascribed to Plato; scholars agree that it was written two or three centuries later.

To the Americans is very loosely based on Horace's ode to the Romans, III, 6.

The Noble Rider and the Sound of Words: A Cento—The cento (the word means "patchwork") is a poem made up of phrases and scraps from another work. It was a popular form in antiquity. The Greek and Roman centos were most often made from the poems of Homer or Virgil—the empress Eudoxia wrote a life of Christ composed entirely of segments of Homer's verse. Except for some brief comic pieces, the form has not been seen for a long time. Every line and sentence in my cento has been constructed from patches of Wallace Stevens' famous essay of the same title. I have always found that essay more than a little obscure and thought that by breaking it into bits and recombining the bits I might make sense of it in verse—even if not quite the sense that Stevens had in mind. I have altered very little, here and there changing or adding a connective, a tense, a punctuation mark. Whenever it came freely to mind and seemed to fit, I have interpolated a line or two from his poetry.

One-Rime Dream is a dramatic monologue; the speaker is the late poet, Henri Coulette.

After Ten Years is an elegy for Coulette, loosely based on a poem by Borges.

Hardy—The story referred to in the octave is family lore but for the most part accepted by the biographers. The doctor set the infant Hardy aside, thinking him stillborn; the midwife (who was probably not yet an old crone) revived him. It was highly unusual in rural Dorset in 1840 for a doctor to be in attendance at a birth; the Hardy family were somewhat more prosperous than their peasant kin and neighbors.

Variation on a Theme is based on Horace's famous ode, III, 30.

INDEX OF TITLES AND FIRST LINES